CITY OF BIRMINGHAM

CARGO SHIPS
A Colour Portfolio

David L. Williams & Richard de Kerbrech

Ian Allan
PUBLISHING

INVENTOR *(previous page)*

(5/1964) T. & J. Harrison (Charente Steamship Co Ltd)
9,171grt; 493ft 4in (150.36m) loa x 63ft 4in (19.30m) beam
C. Connell & Co Ltd, Glasgow
Oil 2SA 8-cyl by Sulzer Bros, Winterthur, Switzerland: 12,600bhp

A new class of refrigerated cargo ship, the *Inventor* was launched on 21 August 1963 with a deadweight tonnage of 10,495. All her holds were served by cranes, while Nos 2 and 3 holds could also be served by her Stülcken heavy lift derrick if required. She sailed on her maiden voyage on 16 May 1964 from Birkenhead to Mombasa. The *Inventor* was an improved version of the earlier *Adventurer* and *Tactician*, which had been built with Sampson posts and derricks in the period before cranes were installed. Like the earlier duo, the *Inventor* was built with split island accommodation, the Mates being housed in the forward block while the engineers were placed abaft around the engine space, this configuration giving her a tanker-like appearance. After 17 years with Harrison's the *Inventor* was sold in 1981 to Penta World Private Ltd of Singapore and renamed *Penta World*. After four more years of service, she arrived at Kaohsiung on 17 May 1985 for demolition. The photograph shows the *Inventor* anchored in a calm waterway during July 1978. *Mick Lindsay*

First published 2007

ISBN (10) 0 7110 3161 4
ISBN (13) 978 0 7110 3161 6

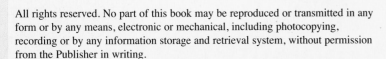

Published by Ian Allan Publishing

an imprint of Ian Allan Publishing Ltd, Hersham, Surrey KT12 4RG.
Printed in England by Ian Allan Printing Ltd, Hersham, Surrey KT12 4RG.

Code: 0701/B

Visit the Ian Allan Publishing website at www.ianallanpublishing.com

Explanatory Notes

Preceding each caption or group of captions is a block of technical and date information relating to the named and featured ship or ships. The layout of this information, is as follows:

The vessel's name, (month and year built);
former names with the (year) in which the name changes occurred;
the vessel's owners;
the vessel's vital statistics: tonnage, length and beam in feet and inches with the equivalent (metric values);
the vessel's builders and shipyard location;
the engine installation, the engine builders and, where known, the horsepower output.

Abbreviations

Throughout, the following abbreviations have been adopted:

ft	feet
grt	gross registered tonnage
hp	high pressure
in	inches
ip	intermediate pressure
loa	length overall
lp	low pressure
m	metres
2SA	Two-stroke Single Acting
2DA	Two-stroke Double Acting
4SA	Four-stroke Single Acting
4DA	Four-stroke Double Acting
bhp	brake horsepower
ihp	indicated horsepower (a calculated horsepower, nominally reckoned as 87% of brake horsepower)
nhp	nominal horsepower
shp	shaft horsepower
cyl	cylinders

Introduction

.While it would be wrong to suggest that transitions in shipping practices have occurred according to precise dates, nevertheless this book could still be said to embrace an era of cargo shipping that spanned from tramp steamers to container ships — extending from the mid-1950s to the early 1970s.

Among the striking characteristics of that period of merchant shipping were the sheer volume and variety of the cargo traffic operating in British waters throughout those years. The British Merchant Navy then still led the world, this being just prior to the commencement of the process of 'flagging-out': transferring ostensibly British ships under the registration of flags-of-convenience states in order to reap tax advantages and circumvent safety and certification standards. Britain's extensive presence on the high seas prior to that was reflected in the form of numerous long-established shipping lines and their countless though instantly recognisable ships, each associated with the conveyance of merchandise from a particular region of the world or along a particular trade route. To name but a few, there were Elder Dempster, Blue Star, Furness Withy, Houlders and Alfred Holts; there were the Bens and Clans and Glens, the 'Citys' of Ellermans, the 'M' boats of Brocklebank and the 'Stans' of Strick. There were also the large cargo fleets operated by major passenger shipping companies, like Cunard, Canadian-Pacific, Union Castle, Shaw Savill and, of course, P&O. In those years, London Docks was described as a 'veritable City of Ships' and each dock complex, each wharf and warehouse along the Thames was known for the cargoes it handled: tea, rice, porcelain and spices from the Orient; tobacco, coffee, leather and sugar from the Caribbean and the Americas; diamonds, fruit, gold and silver from Africa; meat, butter, fruit and timber from the Dominions of the Commonwealth, and so on. And it was much the same at the other great ports of Liverpool, Bristol and Southampton.

As suggested in the opening paragraph, this was, of course, a time of enormous change. Revealed here is a gallery of the ships of that period, a tapestry of great variety — everything from the fast disappearing traditional vessels to some of the emerging new types that were making their older cousins redundant. The term cargo ship applies generically to a broad and multifarious group of different merchant vessels. It includes break-bulk dry, liquid and refrigerated types, also cargo-passenger liners and heavy lift ships, as well as bulk loaders and unitised cargo or container vessels.

It remained the era, though by then it was in a state of decline, of tramp, general trader or charter shipping, the practice of collecting cargos wherever they could be found and delivering them to wherever they were destined,

anywhere in the world. Typically fitted with triple-expansion steam engines prior to World War 2, later tramp ships adopted diesel engines that better suited this mode of operation. Cheaper than cargo liners to maintain in periods of reduced trade, and often laid up idle at anchorages during such conditions, the tramp owner, on the other hand, did not enjoy any of the protections given by the Liner Conferences.

In contrast, cargo liners, sometimes identified as freighters, work regular sailing schedules on fixed routes established under the auspices of Liner Conference rules. In fact, it was the introduction of the cargo liner that brought about the decline of the tramp ship, once the backbone of the British Merchant Service. By offering the benefit of regular arrivals and departures the cargo liner gradually encroached into the tramp's traditional territory, permitting traders to plan their affairs and take greater advantage of favourable market conditions.

At this time, too, break-bulk shipping and conventional cargo handling practices were beginning to give way to specialised systems such as containerisation, while both dry and liquid bulk cargoes were being increasingly loaded and discharged at new, dedicated terminals located away from the old port centres, facilities that were linked to the emerging motorway network. One of the less fortunate consequences of these changes has been the gradual run-down of old dockland areas and their associated rail infrastructure. More recently such decline has been reversed by ambitious commercial and residential dockland developments, though not necessarily for the benefit of the original communities of these districts. Having already lost their specialised employment — the livelihood of docklands families for generations — these communities have been increasingly fragmented and displaced as the modern accommodation erected in their neighbourhoods has become unaffordable. Thus, the period covered by the book was something of a crossroads between the past and the future, both at sea and in the ports.

Both conventional cargo liners and tramps have from four to six holds and may also have one or two 'tween deck stowage areas running along almost the entire length of the ship. Many cargo liners have a small amount of usually high-class passenger accommodation. Some, having cabin spaces for as many as 100 passengers, are designated as cargo-passenger liners. The latter term is a somewhat loose description and some of the ships in this category could arguably be grouped with either cargo ships or passenger ships. The confusion is exacerbated when owners make internal modifications to their ships to suit changing trade conditions; sometimes suppressing accommodation spaces altogether, other times enlarging them.

Equally, many cargo vessels have some spaces allocated for refrigerated produce but there is a distinct type known as the refrigerated ship or reefer whose cargo spaces are predominantly temperature-controlled and insulated for the specialised carriage of fruit, meat and dairy products. To be so designated, the ship must have in excess of 80,000cu ft of refrigerated cargo chambers for the carriage of perishable cargoes.

Another variant of the cargo ship is the heavy-lift cargo liner, which has, in place of all or some conventional derricks and cranes, one or two patented Stülcken derricks capable of lifting loads of up to 300 tons, equipment that generally has superseded earlier forms of heavy-lift deck gear.

The shelter-decker category of cargo vessel was developed to gain additional cargo space by exploiting the open areas available on the shelter deck. There are two forms: the closed shelter deck (CSD) vessel in which the transverse bulkheads are taken right up to the shelter deck (the deck above the main deck), and the open shelter deck (OSD) vessel, where they are taken no higher than the main deck.

During the period covered by the book some companies were still operating wartime-built standard and emergency ships that had reverted to peacetime duties, while others were taking delivery of new dry cargo ships of standard design, such as Austin & Pickersgill's SD-14 series, introduced in the mid-1960s. Simultaneously, the first specially-built all-container or unit/system cargo ships were also starting to make their appearance, their huge metal boxes loaded and unloaded at centres located miles from the sea for conveyance by road and rail to be rapidly and efficiently stowed aboard them by equally novel gantry transporter cranes. The emergence of container ships and modern roll-on roll-off (Ro-Ro) vessels has had the effect of rendering almost redundant many of the traditional cargo vessels presented here, effectively doing to them what they earlier had done to tramp ships.

In parallel with this evolution of cargo-carrying ship types, there has been a trend of increasing the size of ships, exploiting the principle of economy of scale, in parallel with a marked reduction in their numbers. Resulting in a direct depletion of the ships that could be viewed in estuaries and along the tidal rivers, these new vessels have also indirectly set in motion the eradication of other types of port traffic. Commonly fitted with bow and stern thrusters, they are able to dock without the assistance of tugs. Greater capacity fuel stowage tanks have obviated the requirement for much bunkering from fuel barges, while containerisation has all but killed-off the lighterage business on the Thames and elsewhere.

The key feature of cargo ship design, of course, was the type and configuration of the cargo-handling equipment installed aboard each vessel. While home ports in the UK generally offered quayside berths supported by modern cranes, in contrast the process of discharging or loading cargo while overseas often had to be carried out in the roadstead or at an anchorage, sometimes from both sides simultaneously — functions wholly dependent on the ship's own gear.

Conventional deck-mounted cargo-handling equipment comprised derricks attached to masts or samson posts (otherwise known as king posts), powered by winches and arranged in single or multiple units to serve each cargo hold. Heavy-lift Stülcken derricks are used for handling very heavy loads such as locomotives, civil engineering plant, power station equipment and so on. On later vessels cranes have been fitted in place of derricks as they free up deck spaces while they also have the advantage of a better range of movement.

Before concluding this Introduction, mention should be made of the matter of identification of ships' owners. Shipping companies typically have created subsidiaries as the vessel owners beneath a holding or managing company. For means of simplicity, the ship owners stated here are, with few exceptions, those holding or managing concerns, in whose colours the ships were painted, rather than the subsidiaries. For example, Blue Star Line is identified as the owner rather than Union International Co, Union Cold Storage, Frederick Leyland or any other of the many Vestey Group companies. Where appropriate, the caption notes explain the relationships between the various concerns involved with a particular ship.

Once again, much of the pictorial content here has been drawn from the wonderful collection of images taken by the late Kenneth Wightman, depicting a period when British shipping was at its peak, operating in a UK port scene that is now but a distant memory. Besides his pictures, in order to offer the reader a balanced spread of the ships and companies that were then operating, a similar number of the superb colour photographs from the collection assembled by Mick Lindsay (some originally taken by Bill Mitchell) have been included. As with previous titles in this series, it is hoped that the reader will derive pleasure both from the individual images, most taken between 40 and 50 years ago, and the gallery of pictures as a whole, depicting a time now gone by: a time when ships still looked like ships and the quality of life, though tougher through hard toil, was less frantic and less pressurised, affording greater opportunity to enjoy watching ships at work — the mechanical and natural environments in harmony.

David L. Williams and Richard P. de Kerbrech
Isle of Wight, November 2006

ASHBANK

(5/1959) Bank Line
6,452grt; 483ft 4in (147.31m) loa x 62ft 9in
   (19.13m) beam
Harland & Wolff Ltd, Belfast
Oil 2SA 6-cyl (by builder): 6,700bhp

The Bank Line invested heavily in new tonnage during the 1950s and into the 1960s, such that by that time they had one of the largest cargo fleets under the Red Ensign, comprising some 40 or more ships. This picture, taken at Cardiff in October 1971, shows the *Ashbank* in light condition. She was one of the large number of similar vessels built for Bank Line during this period of fleet expansion. Her owners operated an extensive network of worldwide routes, which suggested a tramp shipping operation. However, the Bank Line movements constituted regular services rather than charter voyages. The *Ashbank* was sold to Crest Shipping Limited, Liberia in 1976 and renamed *Newcrest*. Her engines were of the exhaust piston type, constructed by Harland & Wolff. Her sister, the 1961-built *Levernbank*, sank on 11 July 1973 after stranding in thick fog two days earlier, on rocks off Matawani, Peru. *Mick Lindsay*

ERNEBANK

(2/1937) Bank Line
5,388grt; 448ft 5in (136.67m) loa x 57ft 4in
   (17.47m) beam
Harland & Wolff Ltd, Belfast
Oil 4SA 6-cyl (by builder)

A Bank Line ship of an earlier period is the prewar *Ernebank*, photographed in May 1961. Like all the vessels in her owners' fleet, she was a motorship. The Bank Line, more correctly referred to as Andrew Weir Shipping & Trading Co Ltd, was one of the few British companies to survive into the late 1980s — when it joined forces with Shaw Savill to form Bank-Savill Line. The *Ernebank* served her owners in peacetime and wartime, a 26-year career that ended with her breaking up in 1963. *Mick Lindsay*

WAVEBANK

(2/1959) Bank Line
6,327grt; 487ft (148.83m) loa x 62ft 3in (18.98m) beam
William Doxford & Sons (Shipbuilding) Ltd, Sunderland
Oil 2SA 4-cyl (by builder): 4,800bhp

Sister-ship to the *Yewbank*, completed the same year, was Bank Line's *Wavebank*, shown here in ballast in September 1969. The pair were of the closed shelter decker type with 15 derricks of different tonnage capacities, powered by electric winches and serving five main hatches. Aft of the engine room was a deep tank for the carriage of either fuel or vegetable oil. Deadweight tonnage was 12,160 calculated on a closed shelter deck draught of approximately 29ft. Officers and catering staff were accommodated in the main superstructure block, whereas the crew, both deck and engine-room, had cabins in the 'tween decks spaces and in the aft deckhouse. Their engines were of the opposed-piston type. Sold to Tide Shipping Limited, Liberia, in 1976, the *Wavebank* became the *Newtide*, surviving under this identity until 1985 when it is believed she was disposed of for scrap. *Mick Lindsay*

BENARTY

(2/1963) Ben Line

10,294grt; 509ft (155.13m) loa x 66ft 11in (20.39m) beam

Caledon SB & E Co Ltd, Dundee

Oil 6-cyl Sulzer type by D. Rowan & Co, Glasgow: 9,000bhp

Allocated the name of a former Ministry of Transport 'Empire' vessel — another heavy lift ship — that was sold in June 1962, the sixth *Benarty*, ordered for Far East service, was launched on 12 October 1962. Built as a shelter decker, she was equipped with a distinctive Stülcken heavy lift derrick of 180 tons capacity mounted between two transversely splayed derrick posts and operated by twin topping spars connected to the posts. As such she was a unique vessel in the Ben Line fleet of the early 1960s.

In addition she had 5 sets of conventional cargo-lifting derricks, located forward and aft to serve holds on either side of the machinery spaces. This photograph of her, taken in April 1974, shows her turning off the Royal Docks entrance, in Blackwall Reach. In the background, at North Greenwich, is the Delta Wharf. *Kenneth Wightman*

BENCRUACHAN

(6/1946) Ben Line

8,047grt; 482 ft 7in (147.08m) loa x 60 ft 2in (18.34m) beam

J. L. Thompson & Sons Ltd, Sunderland

2 x double-reduction geared steam turbines by Richardsons, Westgarth & Co, West Hartlepool: 7,500shp

Photographed in the hands of PLA tugs in the canal linking the King George V Dock and the Royal Victoria Dock, otherwise known as the 'cut', the steamship *Bencruachan* was among the first of the replacement vessels constructed for the Ben Line after World War 2, to make good the 14 ships that had been lost to enemy action. Launched on 19 October 1945, she was similar to the slightly smaller *Benlawers*, completed two years earlier. The *Bencruachan* remained in service with Ben Line until June 1966 when she was renamed *Annunciation Day* after her sale to Five March Shipping Co SA, Greece. She changed owners again twice in 1974, ultimately becoming the *Demis* for Demis Navigation Co SA, also Greece. A year later she was laid up in Piraeus remaining so until she left the port under tow in March 1979 destined for Split, Yugoslavia where she was broken up by Brodospas. *Kenneth Wightman*

BENMACDHUI
(2/1948) Ben Line
8,047grt; 474 ft 6in (144.62m) loa x 60 ft 4in (18.39m)
  beam
C. Connell & Co Ltd, Glasgow
2 x double-reduction geared steam turbines by D. Rowan
  & Co Ltd, Glasgow: 7,500shp

The *Benmacdhui* was the first of a class of five new steam-powered general dry cargo ships, constructed for Ben Line in the late 1940s, her sisters being, in the order in which they were delivered, the *Benvenue*, *Bencleuch*, *Benavon* and *Benalder*. Launched on 3 June 1947, the *Benmacdhui* served Ben Line for almost 25 years. She was sold for breaking up at Dalmuir from 23 April 1972 by W. H. Arnott, Young & Co Ltd. All the vessels of her class were modified during their careers by the installation of an additional pair of king posts on the fo'c'sle. Their funnels also had modifications incorporated in them, either the addition of a vented front rim or, as in the case of the *Benmacdhui*, seen here with the Gamecock steam tug *Ocean Cock* on her arrival in the Thames, a cone-shaped stove pipe. *Kenneth Wightman*

ANCHISES

(4/1947) Alfred Holt & Co
  (Blue Funnel Line)
7,643grt; 487 ft (148.83m)
  loa x 62 ft 4in (19.01m)
  beam
Caledon S.B. & E. Co Ltd,
  Dundee
Oil 2DA 8-cyl Burmeister &
  Wain by J.G. Kincaid &
  Co, Greenock: 6,800bhp

Alfred Holt & Company's 'A' class ships, of which a total of 27 of various marks were built, were sturdy workhorses built for the Far East routes, all based on a prewar Glen Line design. Their engines, manufactured under licence, were of the exhaust piston type. Initially, they performed well on diesel fuel but from the early 1950s problems arose after they were adapted to run on heavy fuel or boiler oil. The potential cost savings of this modification were more than outweighed by breakdowns and the costs of increased maintenance and replacement parts. The emergence of improved cylinder oils remedied the situation, extending the life of this class of ships well into the 1970s. Photographed in the Royal Docks, London in April 1968, this is Blue Funnel Line's *Anchises* registered with the Ocean Steamship Co. Her claim to fame was that she came under attack from Chinese Nationalist bombers in the Huangpo River on 21 June 1949, while bound from Woosung to Shanghai. Damaged aft, she settled in shallow water with her engine room flooded but was later refloated and repaired at Kobe, Japan. In January 1973 she was renamed *Alcinous*, heralding a period of movement between various companies of the Holt Group. Her end came in September 1974 when she was sold for breaking up at Kaohsiung, Taiwan. *Kenneth Wightman*

ANTILOCHUS

(1949) Alfred Holt & Co (Blue Funnel Line)
7,702grt; 487ft (148.83m) loa x 62ft 4in
  (19.01m) beam
Harland & Wolff, Belfast
Oil 2DA 8-cyl Burmeister & Wain
  (by builder): 6,800bhp

Unlike the *Anchises*, which was an 'A' class Mk I type, the refrigerated cargo ship *Antilochus* was a unit of the follow-on Mk II variant. She is viewed here from under the bow of Glen Line's *Monmouthshire*, in London's Royal Albert Dock, placing the date of this picture between 1957 and 1963, when the latter ship's name was changed. Like her contemporaries, the *Antilochus* was fitted for carrying Muslim pilgrims from Malaya and Indonesia to Jeddah. Cargo-handling gear on this class included two jumbo derricks, one of 50 tons lift, and they had deep tanks for palm oil, latex or other liquid cargoes. After transferring to Elder Dempster in 1975, she moved on two years later to Gulf (Shipowners) Ltd of London for whom she was renamed *Orient*. The former *Antilochus* was broken up at Gadani Beach, Karachi, Pakistan, from early May 1978. *Kenneth Wightman*

JASON

(1/1950) Alfred Holt & Co (China Mutual S.N. Co Ltd.)

10,160grt; 552ft 6in (168.39m) loa x 69ft 4in (21.13m) beam

Swan Hunter & Wigham Richardson, Wallsend-on-Tyne

3 x double-reduction geared steam turbines by Wallsend Slipway Co Ltd, Wallsend-on-Tyne: 15,000shp

Photographed at Liverpool, with what is thought to be the same owner's *Telemachus* ex *Teiresias* ex *Silverelm* berthed beyond her, the *Jason* was the second of a class of four ships, designated the 'H' class after the lead vessel, the *Helenus*, completed in October 1949. Launched on 9 June 1949, the *Jason* commenced her maiden voyage, bound for Brisbane, Australia, on 19 February 1950. Slightly larger than, and successors to, the earlier 'P'-class, with the addition of refrigerated cargo spaces, the other ships of the 'H' class were the *Hector* and *Ixion*. All four offered limited first-class accommodation for 30 to 35 passengers until 1964 when their cabin spaces were removed and they became dedicated cargo ships. Unlike other Blue Funnel ships of this period, the 'H' class carried no samson posts on the fo'c'sle or poop. The *Jason* was sold to Taiwanese shipbreakers in 1972 and broken up at Kaohsiung from that May. *Kenneth Wightman*

BRISBANE STAR
(1/1937) Blue Star Line
11,147grt; 542 ft 11in
  (165.47m) loa x 70 ft
  3in (21.41m) beam
Cammell Laird & Co Ltd,
  Birkenhead
2 x Oil 2SA 10-cyl by
  Sulzer Bros Ltd,
  Winterthur, Switzerland

One of a large group of similar twin-screw refrigerated motorships, designated as 'Empire Food Ships', the *Brisbane Star*'s sisters were the *Imperial*, *Empire*, *New Zealand*, *Australia*, *Dunedin*, *Sydney* and *Melbourne Stars*, all completed prior to the outbreak of World War 2, and four of which were lost during that conflict. Here berthed at Southampton's New Docks in the late 1950s, with the Cunard transatlantic liner *Queen Elizabeth* and express mail ships of Union Castle beyond her stern, the *Brisbane Star* had a chequered career not without its own excitement during the war. She was launched on 16 September 1936 and completed for Union Cold Storage Co Ltd early in the following year. Managed by Blue Star Line, she was transferred to Frederick Leyland & Co in 1942. On 12 August of that year, while part of the notorious 'Pedestal' convoy bound for Malta, she was attacked in the Skuki Channel, south of Sicily, and damaged by an aircraft-launched torpedo. Despite severe damage to her bow, she arrived at Valletta two days later, her valuable cargo helping to relieve the besieged island. Repaired and returned to service, after the war's end, in 1950, her owners changed again when she passed to Lamport & Holt Ltd, finally coming under the direct ownership of Blue Star Line in 1959. Four years later she was renamed *Enea* after she was sold to Margalante Compania Naviera SA, Liberia. Within three months she was sold again, to Japanese ship-breakers, arriving at Osaka in October 1963 for demolition to commence. *Kenneth Wightman*

FREMANTLE STAR

(4/1960) Blue Star Line
8,403grt; 519ft (158.18m) loa x 70ft 3in
  (21.41m) beam
Cammell Laird & Co (S.B. & Eng.) Ltd,
  Birkenhead
Oil 2SA 8-cyl by Harland & Wolff, Belfast:
  13,300bhp

The *Fremantle Star* was an open shelter deck
type of cargo ship with refrigerated cargo
spaces. Her motor engines were of the exhaust
piston type. Her cargo-handling equipment
comprised derricks forward plus eight cranes,
four each forward and aft of her bridge and
accommodation structure. Launched for Blue

Star Line on 30 December 1959, she was transferred to Lamport & Holt Ltd in 1964, only to revert to Blue Star ownership a year later. In 1975, as
part of further changes to the fleets of Blue Star companies, she was placed under the control of Blue Star Ship Management Ltd. Four years later
she was sold to Caxton Maine Enterprise Corporation and renamed *Catrina*, although management remained with Blue Star Ship Management.
Within the year her career came to an end when she was sold for breaking up in Taiwan, arriving at Kaohsiung on 30 November 1979.
Kenneth Wightman

SCOTTISH STAR

(12/1950) Blue Star Line
10,174grt; 505ft 6in (154.06m) loa x 70ft 2in
  (21.38m) beam
Fairfield S. B. & Eng. Co Ltd, Glasgow
2 x Oil 2SA 5-cyl Doxford (by builder):
  11,600bhp

Launched on 15 May 1950, the refrigerated
cargo ship *Scottish Star* was a sister to the
English Star delivered by the same builders.
They were of the closed type of shelter deck
cargo ship. Their engines were of the opposed-
piston type. Ownership was transferred to
Lamport & Holt in 1964 but reverted to
Blue Star Line a year later. Two years later, on
6 June 1967, the *Scottish Star* was trapped in
the Great Bitter Lakes, in the Suez Canal,

when it was blockaded during the Arab-Israeli War. Unable to escape, she rapidly deteriorated and was declared a constructive total loss in September 1969. Ownership at this point transferred to the Standard Steamship Owners Mutual War Risk Association in London. She finally left the Canal, under tow for Port Said, Egypt, on 30 May 1975 and she was immediately sold to Greek owners complete with her cargo which had still not been discharged after 8 years. Of course, comprising fruit, bales of greasy wool and jarrah timber, much of it was ruined. Renamed *Kavo Yerakas* she was taken in tow to Piraeus, where, on her arrival that August, her cargo was finally unloaded. After 4 more years laid up she was sold to Spanish shipbreakers in June 1979, almost half of her life having been lost through enforced idleness. *Kenneth Wightman*

SYDNEY STAR
(3/1936) Blue Star Line
11,219grt; 542ft 10in
(165.44m) loa x 70ft 5in
(21.47m) beam
Harland & Wolff, Belfast
2 x Oil 2DA 6-cyl
(by builder)

Another Empire Food Ship that survived the War, the *Sydney Star* is here seen berthed, probably in the London Docks, in June 1966. Completed for Frederick Leyland, she was damaged by a German E-boat on 24 July 1941 while in convoy to Malta where she arrived the same day. She was dry-docked in Valletta for repairs. In 1950 she was transferred to Blue Star Line Limited and continued to serve these owners until 1967, a total of 31 years of service for the Vestey Group. Her new Greek owners, Embajada Compania Naviera SA, gave her the temporary name *Kent*. Sold on to Taiwanese shipbreakers, she arrived at Kaohsiung on 11 August 1967 for demolition to commence. The later *Wellington Star* and *Auckland Star* were similar but improved versions, equipped with an additional pair of derricks forward. *Kenneth Wightman*

ULSTER STAR
(7/1959) Blue Star Line
10,413grt; 519ft 3in (158.26m) loa x
    70ft 4in (21.44m) beam
Harland & Wolff, Belfast
Oil 2SA 6-cyl (by builder):
    10,000bhp

Like other Blue Star ships, the *Ulster Star* moved between various companies within the Vestey Group throughout her career. Completed for Blue Star Line, she was transferred to Lamport & Holt in 1964, though management remained with Blue Star. In the following year she returned to Blue Star Line ownership, remaining so until 1975 when Blue Star Ship Management Ltd were appointed as her managers. Four years later she was sold for breaking up by Nan Hor Steel Enterprise Co, Taiwan and arrived at Kaohsiung on 13 August 1979 with scrapping commencing shortly thereafter. The *Ulster Star* is seen here at a somewhat unusual location for Blue Star, berthed in Newhaven docks in November 1977. *Ken Lowe*

NUDDEA
(8/1954) British India Line
8,596grt; 514ft 3in (156.74m) loa x 67ft 2in (20.47m)
  beam
Barclay, Curle & Co Ltd, Glasgow
3 x steam turbines, 2 double reduction-geared HP &
  1 single-reduction geared LP (by builder): 11,275shp

Arriving off Tilbury Landing Stage in August 1966, the *Nuddea* can be seen with two vessels of the Soviet flag *Mikhail Kalinin* class moored behind her. Lead ship of a class of cargo ships of 28,000cu ft refrigerated capacity, her sister vessels were the *Nyanza*, *Nardana* and *Nowshera*. Displaced first by imminent containerisation on the UK to Australia service, the *Nuddea* was moved from 1967 to the Japan to Persian Gulf route, subsequently passing to P&O ownership without change of name, in April 1972. Less than a year later, in February 1973, she fell the victim of rapidly rising fuel costs and was sold for breaking up in Taiwan. *Kenneth Wightman*

MAHRONDA

(3/1947) Brocklebank Line
8,495grt; 504ft 7in (153.80m) loa x 62ft
  8in (19.10m) beam
William Hamilton & Co Ltd, Port Glasgow
2 x double-reduction geared steam turbines
  by D. Rowan & Co, Glasgow: 6,800shp

A third postwar new-building and later derivative of the *Magdapur*, the *Mahronda* was launched by the same shipyard on 10 October 1946 and was a sister ship to the *Malabar*. This ship replaced another of the same name that was sunk off Portuguese East Africa (Mozambique) during 1942. The company had sustained heavy losses to its fleet during World War 2 and by 1942 only 11 ships remained of a prewar fleet of 25. The *Mahronda* went on to give some 23 years service to Brocklebank's before being sold to Cypriot interests and renamed *Lucky*. She arrived at Split on 17 December 1970 where she was scrapped. This view is of her approaching the Royal Group of Docks with a Gamecock tug in attendance. *Kenneth Wightman*

MAWANA
(9/1958) Brocklebank Line
8,744grt; 497ft (151.46m) loa x 63ft 5in (19.33m) beam
William Hamilton & Co Ltd, Port Glasgow
2 x double-reduction geared steam turbines by D. Rowan
& Co, Glasgow: 8,000shp

By the time the *Mawana* was launched on 3 July 1958 no fewer than 14 new ships had been built in the postwar period, bringing the Brocklebank company back up to its prewar fleet size. The *Mawana*, along with her sister the *Makrana*, were further improvements of the earlier *Magdapur* design, fitted with three sets of bi-pod masts for cargo handling. She was sold to Greek interests during 1971 and renamed the *Aegis Legend* remaining so until scrapped in Japan in 1974. This photograph of her taken on 23 June 1966 is thought to show her underway in the River Thames and shows a traditional cargo ship before the introduction of containerisation. *Kenneth Wightman*

MARTAND

(6/1939) Brocklebank Line

8,007grt; 494ft 10in (150.80m) loa x 62ft
8in (19.10m) beam

William Hamilton & Co Ltd, Port
Glasgow

3 x single-reduction geared steam turbines
by D. Rowan & Co, Glasgow

This photograph of the prewar *Martand*, taken sometime during the early 1960s, shows her alongside at 101 berth in Southampton's Western docks. Having been one of Brocklebank's fortunate survivors from the war, she was wrecked and sank at Ulubaria in the Hooghly River in May 1964. Loaded with a cargo of manganese ore, kynite ore, jute, shellac and other produce destined for Middlesbrough and Continental ports, she grounded on a sandbar in the river after fouling an anchor. With her engine room and stokehold flooded, she broke in two on 13 May, two days after the initial accident. Abandoned half-submerged, she was declared a constructive total loss. Of interest in this view is a member of the crew painting the ship's side with a roller from the starboard lifeboat! *Mick Lindsay*

MATANGI
(10/1961) ex *Port St. Lawrence* (1975)
 Brocklebank Line
10,486grt; 500ft 2in (152.44m) loa x 67ft
 11in (20.70m) beam
Harland & Wolff, Belfast
Oil 2SA 7-cyl Burmeister & Wain
 (by builder): 11,500bhp

The *Matangi* started life as Port Line's *Port St Lawrence* and was built as a pair with the *Port Alfred* for that company's Australian and New Zealand trades. As a conventional refrigerated cargo ship she served her intended trade route for some 15 years but by 1976 changes in ownership and management were manifesting themselves. Port Line transmogrified into Blueport Management and then came under the Trafalgar House Investments holding group. The *Port St. Lawrence* was transferred to the Cunard Steam Ship Co and then to its subsidiary, T. & J. Brocklebank, to be renamed *Matangi*. She was only to be with them for six years — she was then sold to a Maltese company, Armier Shipping Co, and renamed *Nordave* in 1982. After only a few months she arrived on 30 April 1983 at Gadani Beach, Karachi where she was broken up. Here the *Matangi* is photographed inbound in Southampton Water during September 1977. Even though she is in Brocklebank colours, her style and design betray her Port Line origins. *Mick Lindsay*

BEAVERCOVE
(9/1947) ex *Maplecove* (1956) ex
   Beavercove (1952) Canadian Pacific Line
9,824grt; 497ft 6in (151.64m) loa x 64ft 4in
   (19.61m) beam
Lithgows, Port Glasgow
2 x steam turbines connected to electric
   motor by C. A. Parsons & Co, Newcastle:
   9,000shp

Last of the quartet of turbo-electric cargo liners introduced by Canadian Pacific on its transatlantic service from 1946, the *Beavercove* is seen turning off the entrance to the King George V dock. Port of London Authority vessels can be seen in the background as well as two red London buses, heading along Woolwich Manor Way to cross the bascules over the entrance lock. Like her sister *Beaverdell*, the *Beavercove* was renamed for her owners' Pacific service, becoming the *Maplecove* in July 1952. That December she was damaged in a severe storm, losing her rudder and requiring the assistance of a tug in order to safely reach Vancouver. The following year she returned to London to resume transatlantic operations, reverting to the name *Beavercove* in December 1956. Seven years later, on 14 August 1963, she was sold to the Italian company Giacomo Costa for its Genoa to South America cargo service under the name *Giovanna Costa*. *Kenneth Wightman*

BEAVERDELL
(2/1946) ex *Mapledell* (1956) ex
Beaverdell (1952) Canadian Pacific
Line
9,901grt; 497ft 6in (151.64m) loa x
64ft 4in (19.61m) beam
Lithgows, Port Glasgow
2 x steam turbines connected to
electric motor by C. A. Parsons &
Co, Newcastle: 9,000shp

The *Beaverdell* was launched on 27 August 1945 as one of a quartet of single-screw turbo-electric cargo ships for Canadian Pacific's transatlantic route, the others being the *Beaverglen*, *Beaverlake* and *Beavercove*. They were replacements for five earlier Beaver-class ships lost during the war. The *Beaverdell* sailed on her maiden voyage from Liverpool on 28 February 1946 as a cargo-only vessel with six holds comprising 163,318cu ft of refrigerated space and 434,394cu ft of general cargo space. All cargo handling was by six pairs of goal-post style Samson posts. On 28 August 1952 she was renamed *Mapledell* and switched to the company's Pacific service. Two years later she returned to the Atlantic run and was once more renamed *Beaverdell* on 21 December 1956. Latterly she operated from London until 11 January 1963 when she was sold to Giacomo Costa Fu Andrea and renamed *Luisa Costa*. By 1971 she had become surplus to requirements and was scrapped at La Spezia. This photograph taken on 24 June 1958 shows the *Beaverdell* swinging on her anchor. Her goal-post derricks are clearly highlighted in this view. *Kenneth Wightman*

CLAN MACDOUGALL
(5/1944) Houston Line
9,710grt; 505ft 6in (154.08m)
   loa x 64ft 8in (19.71m) beam
Greenock Dockyard Co,
   Greenock
2 x Oil 4SA 10-cyl Burmeister
   & Wain by J. G. Kinkaid &
   Co, Greenock: 11,100bhp

As with many other ships of the Clan Line (or the 'Scots' Navy' as it was often referred to), the *Clan Macdougall* was built at the company's preferred yard of Greenock Dockyard. Ironically, given that it was wartime, she was fitted with Kinkaid B&W diesels built under license. Innovation had to be the order of the day as spares were hard to come by, for the Copenhagen 'licensor' of the machinery was then under German occupation! These engines gave her a creditable speed of 16 knots. Clan Line's routes were diverse — from the UK to the Red Sea ports, Africa, Mauritius, India, Ceylon (Sri Lanka) and Pakistan, also from the UK to Australia and Tasmania. In the late 1950s she was switched to the Clan Line subsidiary, the Houston Line (London) Ltd, to trade between the USA and South and East African ports. She was scrapped in Taiwan during 1971 having been renamed *Vrysi* for her last voyage to the breakers. This picture of the *Clan Macdougall* was taken in August 1971 during her last year in service. The two-island mates' and engineers' accommodation may be clearly seen. *Mick Lindsay*

CLAN MACINTYRE

(3/1952) Clan Line
6,560grt; 471 ft (143.56m) loa x 60ft 8in
(18.49m) beam
John Brown & Co, Clydebank
Oil 2SA 6-cyl Doxford (by builder):
5,650bhp

One of a trio of new motorships for the Clan Line, the *Clan Macintyre* was built by John Brown as was her sister *Clan Macintosh*, while the third ship, *Clan Macinnes*, was also constructed on the Clyde, in her case by the Greenock Dockyard Company. Each had accommodation for 12 passengers and was driven by a single Doxford opposed-piston engine. In 1975 the *Clan Macintyre* was transferred to the King Line before being sold to Renown Bay Shipping Co Ltd of Panama and renamed *Eastern Express*. Whilst trading with the latter company, on 22 December 1979, she was wrecked half a mile south of Marina di Carrara in Italy while bound for Sardinia. Driven ashore in severe weather, she subsequently sank. In this view, she is shown moored abreast another Clan Line vessel in the Albion Basin at Birkenhead. *Kenneth Wightman*

CLAN MACLAREN
(12/1946) Clan Line
6,365grt; 466ft (142.04m) loa x
   60ft 11in (18.57m) beam
Greenock Dockyard Co, Greenock
Oil 2SA 6-cyl Doxford by Barclay,
   Curle & Co, Glasgow: 5,650bhp

When the *Clan Maclaren* was launched on 25 September 1946 she was one of a postwar trio destined for general cargo work, which sported three pairs of goal-post type derricks. Notwithstanding her single engine and relatively low horsepower, she could maintain a service speed of 15-16 knots. Between 1963 and 1968 she was transferred to Hector Whaling Ltd of Glasgow, only to be returned to Clan Line from 1968 to 1976. After a total service of 30 years she was sold to Seymour Shipping Ltd of Panama and renamed *Seemoor* for her last year in trading. She was then sold for demolition and arrived at Gadani Beach, Karachi for scrapping. This photograph of the *Clan Maclaren*, taken in May 1964, is thought to show her at Rotterdam with the tug *Turkije* assisting her to berth. Though taken in a foreign port, this fine view of a classic British cargo ship warranted inclusion here. So, too, a small number of other views elsewhere depict British cargo vessels abroad. *Kenneth Wightman*

CLAN URQUHART
(1/1944) Houston Line
9,726grt; 500ft 6in (152.55m) loa x 65ft 10in
  (20.07m) beam
Greenock Dockyard Co, Greenock
Triple expansion 6-cyl steam reciprocating &
  double-reduction geared LP steam turbine by
  J. G. Kinkaid & Co, Greenock: 1,283nhp

The *Clan Urquhart* was a wartime product of her builders, launched on 20 June 1943. Although ordered by Clan Line, upon her completion she entered Government service from 1944 to 1946. She benefited from reliable twin-screw combination machinery and had a large deadweight tonnage capacity of 10,198. For 14 years from 1946 she was operated by Clan Line on her intended service but from 1960 until 1966 she was transferred to Clan Line's subsidiary, the Houston Line (London) Ltd. After only 22 years service she had become surplus to requirements, having been replaced by newer tonnage, and arrived in Taiwan on 8 April 1966 for demolition. This photograph, believed to have been taken in the early 1960s, clearly shows her rather dated wartime appearance. *Mick Lindsay*

ANDRIA

(2/1948) ex *Silverbriar* (1951) Cunard Line
7,228grt; 503ft 4in (153.42m) loa x 64ft 11in (19.79m)
  beam
J. L. Thompson & Sons Ltd, Sunderland
3 x double-reduction geared steam turbines by Parsons
  Marine Steam Turbines, Newcastle: 8,800shp

The turbine steamships *Andria* and her sister *Alsatia*
were originally built for the Silver Line Ltd as the
Silverbriar and *Silverplane* respectively. Each had
accommodation for 12 passengers and they were
employed carrying cargo and passengers on a round-the-
world service. Frequently they operated in conjunction
with ships of Netherlands companies under what was known as the Silver-Java-Pacific Line. These vessels were quite distinctive, if not unique, for
ships of their type and size, having two squat funnels and a well-raked stem. The forward funnel was, in fact, a dummy, housing the captain's
accommodation as well as the ship's radio room, chartroom, wheelhouse and radar installation. Both were purchased by the Cunard Line in 1951
and operated out of London or Liverpool to the Eastern Seaboard of Canada continuing to the Gulf ports of the southern USA. The *Andria* was sold
to China Union Lines, Taipei, in February 1963 and renamed *Union Faith*. Six years later, on 7 April 1969, she sank in the River Mississippi at New
Orleans after being engulfed in flames following a collision with an oil barge. Twenty-five Chinese crew and the American river pilot were killed.
This full broadside view of the *Andria* captures her attractive profile, a postwar design way ahead of its time! *Mick Lindsay*

ARABIA

(7/1955) ex *Castilian* (1966) ex *City of Peterborough* (1964) ex *Castilian* (1963) Cunard Line
3,803grt; 377ft 2in (114.96m) loa x 53ft 5in (62.28m)
  beam
Alexander Stephen & Sons Ltd, Glasgow
Triple expansion 3-cyl steam reciprocating & double-
  reduction geared LP steam turbine by Central Marine
  Eng. Works, Hartlepool: 3,500ihp

Originally built for Westcott & Laurence Lines Ltd
(Ellerman & Papayanni Lines), as the *Castilian* she was
probably one of the last vessels to be installed with
steam reciprocating and low pressure turbine
combination machinery, as late as 1955. This together
with the boiler room was positioned right aft, giving the
ship the appearance of an oil tanker rather than a cargo
ship. She was renamed in 1963 as the *City of
Peterborough* in line with the Ellerman Line's system of

nomenclature. However, she only retained this name for three years before being chartered to the Cunard Line and renamed *Arabia*. With Cunard for only a short time, she inherited the name of a 1947-built 8,720 gross ton cargo ship sold in March 1963. The *Arabia* reverted to Ellerman that same year and was once more renamed *Castilian*, operating with the company for another five years until sold to Maldives

Shipping Limited as the *Maldive Freedom* in 1971. She was scrapped at Gadani Beach, Karachi in 1977. Given the brevity of her interlude with Cunard, this view of the *Arabia* taken in 1966 is most unusual, if not unique. It shows clearly the early application of corporate branding, with the Cunard Line's name boldly painted on the ship's side. *Mick Lindsay*

PHRYGIA
(3/1955) Cunard Line
3,534grt; 348ft (106.07m)
  loa x 49ft 10in (15.19m)
  beam
William Hamilton & Co,
  Port Glasgow
Oil 2SA 4-cyl by
  D. Rowan & Co,
  Glasgow: 3,600bhp

A sister of the *Pavia* and *Lycia*, the *Phrygia* and her sisters could be switched from the North American to the UK to the Mediterranean cargo service as trading patterns dictated. They had a deadweight tonnage of 4,400 and a refrigerated capacity of 8,000cu ft. As a matter of interest, they were among the earliest motor vessels owned by Cunard, there being only four in total in an almost all steamship company in 1960! Another unique feature of the *Phrygia* and her sisters was that their two masts could be telescoped to enable them to pass under the bridges of the Manchester Ship Canal. The *Phrygia* was to have an all too short operational career with Cunard for she was sold in 1965 to Firovnes SA of Greece and renamed *Dimitris M* with whom she traded until 1974 before being sold again, to Fah Mar SA of Panama as the *Asia Developer*. She changed ownership yet again that year to become the *Fong Chi* of the Shun Fong Mar SA, Panama for her final voyage to Kaohsiung, Taiwan where she capsized on 15 February 1975. Refloated that October, demolition continued into 1976. The photograph of the *Phrygia* shows her entering the lock of the Royal Albert Dock in August 1964 with a Ship Towage tug in attendance. The photographer has framed the view by standing under the docks road bridge. *Kenneth Wightman*

FIAN

(4/1964) Elder Dempster Line
7,683grt; 465ft (141.73m) loa x 62ft 3in (18.97m)
  beam
Lithgows Ltd, Port Glasgow
Oil 2SA 5-cyl Sulzer by Fairfield-Rowan Ltd,
  Glasgow: 7,400bhp

The *Fian* was launched on 15 October 1963 and was
the last of a group of six similar sister ships known as
the 'F' group that followed on from the successful
design of their precursors, the 'D' class, namely the
Daru, *Degema* and *Dixcove*. Four of the group,
including the *Fian*, were built by Lithgows of Port
Glasgow — a healthy order for its day! A feature of
this quartet was that, in preference to mild steel,
Lithgows used a light alloy for the superstructure
which weighed only about 70 tons. The weight saving,
of some 100 tons, permitted a corresponding increase
in the ships' deadweight cargo. After only 13 years of
trading, the *Fian* was sold to the South East Asia
Shipping Co (Pvt) Ltd of Bombay and renamed
Mahapriya. She was eventually scrapped at Bombay
from 12 October 1982. The view shows the *Fian*'s
fine underwater hull form whilst in No 5 Drydock
at Liverpool during March 1970. *Mick Lindsay*

FOURAH BAY
(12/1961) Elder Dempster
Line
7,704grt; 465ft (141.73m) loa
x 62ft 3in (18.97m) beam
Scotts S.B. & E. Co,
Greenock
Oil 2SA 5-cyl by Sulzer,
Winterthur: 7,400bhp

Launched on 7 September 1961, two years earlier than the four Lithgows-built ships, the *Fourah Bay* was the lead vessel of the 'F' group of ships that marked a zenith in the company's postwar rebuilding programme. Elder Dempster, whose ships — commonly referred to as 'the monkey boats' — served West Africa from the UK, had sustained a massive loss of 25 ships during World War 2. The *Fourah Bay* was sold during the 1970s for further trading to Cypriot owners and renamed *Alexander Faith*, later changed to *Magda Josefina*. Her final name was *Lemina*, bestowed upon her in 1984 for the voyage to Gadani Beach, Karachi where she was scrapped. The photograph shows the *Fourah Bay* berthed alongside at Liverpool in July 1975 towards the end of her service with Elder Dempster. Note that her name is also prominently displayed athwartships at the rear of her superstructure. Moored forward of her, to the left of the picture, is the 1958–built *Daru* of the same company. *Mick Lindsay*

FORCADOS

(11/1963) Elder Dempster Line
7,689grt; 465ft (141.73m) loa x
62ft 3in (18.97m) beam
Lithgows Ltd, Port Glasgow
Oil 2SA 5-cyl Sulzer by Fairfield-
Rowan Ltd, Glasgow: 7,400bhp

When the *Forcados* was launched at Port Glasgow on 24 March 1963, she was the first of a quartet of similar vessels ordered from Lithgows, the others being the *Fian*, *Falaba* and *Fulani*. Essentially single-screw general cargo liners of the closed shelter deck type with a deadweight tonnage of 8,150, they were used on the West African trade. For cargo handling the *Forcados* was equipped with 19 derricks: one of 80 tons and two of 30 tons lift, four of 15 tons lift, two of 12½ tons, four of 7½ tons and six of 5 tons. After only 12 years in service she was sold in 1975 to Greek owners and renamed the *Cam Ayous*. She was sold on again in 1981 and renamed *Copper Trader* before being scrapped in Karachi during 1983. This photograph of the *Forcados* at Liverpool was taken in June 1975. *Mick Lindsay*

FREETOWN
(2/1964) Elder Dempster Lines
7,689grt; 465ft (141.73m) loa x
    62ft 3in (18.97m) beam
William Hamilton & Co, Port
    Glasgow
Oil 2SA 5-cyl by Fairfield-
    Rowan Ltd, Glasgow:
    7,400bhp

The *Freetown* was to fare rather better than her 'F' class contemporaries by serving with Elder Dempster for 15 years before being sold on. She was launched on 19 September 1963 only a month before her sister *Fian*, in her case at the former William Hamilton yard, which had been taken over by Lithgows. Like the others in her group her 19 derricks were operated via the three bi-pod style masts that found favour in the 'F' group design. She was sold to Singapore interests in 1978 and renamed the *Panseptos*. She was sold again two years later in 1980 and renamed the *Cherry Ruby*. She was scrapped during January 1982. This view of the *Freetown*, taken during July 1966, when the ship was only three years old, shows her derricks being 'topped off' ready for stowing. It is thought that it shows her on the River Thames. Other vessels of this class were the *Falaba* and *Fulani*. *Kenneth Wightman*

PATANI

(8/1954) Elder Dempster Lines
6,183grt; 449ft 11in (137.13m) loa x
    60ft 4in (18.39m) beam
Scotts S.B. & E. Co, Greenock
Oil 2SA 4-cyl (by builder): 2,800bhp

The *Patani*, along with her sister the *Perang*, demonstrated Elder Dempster's continuing commitment to diesel propulsion for its ships even though the two sisters could only manage a service speed of 11 knots! Launched as a general cargo vessel on 22 April 1954, the *Patani* with her sister would influence the design and improvement of later classes and groups of cargo ships in the company, notably the succeeding 'D' class of ships. They were completed with a squat motorship funnel, just above the height of the bridge, which, with their short masts permitted them to transit the Manchester Ship Canal. Later, in 1964, the funnel was heightened. In October 1972 she was sold to Hong Kong owners, Globe Navigation Limited, and renamed *Patwari* with registry at Mogadishu, Somali Republic. Less than six years later she was broken up at Gadani Beach, Karachi from February 1978. The accompanying photograph, taken in October 1967, shows her berthed with other unidentified vessels. The *Patani*'s funnel is painted in the colours of the Guinea Gulf Line Ltd, an Elder Dempster subsidiary that operated from the Brunswick Dock at Liverpool. The emblem at her bows clearly reveals her Elder Dempster connection. *Kenneth Wightman*

CHANGUINOLA

(9/1957) Elders & Fyffes
6,283grt; 411ft 3in (125.35m)
loa x 56ft 10in (17.32m)
beam
Alexander Stephen & Sons
Ltd, Glasgow
2 x double-reduction geared
steam turbines (by builder):
9,000shp

The *Changuinola* was the first in a series of four Fyffes banana boats built at Linthouse, Glasgow. The trade to the Cameroons in West Africa, which had become a major producer, necessitated a different design of ship from the earlier *Matina* (q.v.) whose draught was too deep to cross the river bar prior to arrival at Tiko, the loading port. Thus, shallower-draught turbine vessels were developed to a suitable design, of which *Changuinola* was one, for introduction into this service. The others in the group were the *Chirripo* completed in late 1957, joined by the *Chicanoa* in spring of 1958 and the *Chuscal* in 1961. All had a service speed of 18 knots, resulting in an improvement to the voyage time. In 1970 the *Changuinola* was transferred to Empresa Hondurena (United Fruit Co) as the *Omoa*. She traded in the Caribbean for a further five years before being disposed of, arriving at Dalmuir, Scotland on 6 April 1975 for scrapping. In this photograph the *Changuinola* is moored alongside the Dock Head at Southampton during September 1965. Besides her refrigerated cargo of bananas she originally had accommodation for 12 passengers. *Kenneth Wightman*

GOLFITO

(12/1949) Elders & Fyffes
8,740grt; 447ft 4in (136.35m) loa x 62ft 4in (19.00m) beam
Alexander Stephen & Sons Ltd, Glasgow
4 x double-reduction geared steam turbines (by builder): 10,500shp

The *Golfito* was originally constructed to run between New York and Central American banana ports in accordance with the holding company's, United Fruit Co, schedules rather than those of Elders & Fyffes. As such, following her maiden voyage from Avonmouth on 14 December 1949, she was received with some ceremony at the small Pacific port in Costa Rica after which she was named. Although the *Golfito* could carry 100 passengers, her original route failed because of falling passenger traffic. British currency regulations at the time required United Fruit Company to pay for her in sterling but declining revenues from her New York to Central America service undermined this. Subsequently, she was placed with the *Matina* working between Jamaica and, at first, Rotterdam, later Southampton or Avonmouth. Later, she made regular sailings from Southampton to Jamaica via Trinidad along with her consort *Camito*. The *Golfito* was scrapped at Faslane, Scotland in 1972. In this bow view of her, taken in 1956, she is being assisted through the entrance to the Empress Dock, Southampton by a Red Funnel tug. *Kenneth Wightman*

MATINA
(11/1946) Elders & Fyffes
6,801grt; 443ft (135.03m) loa
    x 57ft 7in (17.55m) beam
Alexander Stephen & Sons
    Ltd, Glasgow
3 x double-reduction geared
    Parsons steam turbines
    (by builder): 8,800shp

The third Fyffes vessel to bear the name the *Matina*, the order for this, the first postwar ship to be delivered to the fleet, marked a return to the Stephen shipyard by the company. The *Matina* was a remarkable vessel of her type, incorporating numerous design improvements and representing a distinct upgrade on previous Fyffes ships. She was the first turbine vessel to join the fleet and had a much larger capacity than her predecessors, along with a service speed of 17½ knots. Furthermore, she had a newer arrangement of refrigeration apparatus installed. The *Matina* had a banana capacity for 170,000 stems and could carry 12 passengers. As previously noted she ran for a time in consort with the larger *Golfito* between Jamaica and Southampton or Avonmouth. Her career ended in 1968 when she was demolished at Bruges. This photograph, taken at Southampton sometime earlier, shows that despite her wartime genesis, when practicality and simplicity were more immediate considerations, she was radical enough to have been built with a raked stem and cruiser stern. *Richard de Kerbrech*

CITY OF BEDFORD

(11/1950) Ellerman Lines

7,341grt; 484ft 10in (147.78m) loa x 61ft 10in (18.85m) beam

Alexander Stephen & Sons Ltd, Glasgow

3 x single-reduction geared steam turbines (by builder): 6,050shp

When the *City of Bedford* was launched on 14 June 1950 she was one of a group of four sisters to join the fast growing postwar fleet of the richest shipowner in the UK at the time. Her consorts were the *City of Birkenhead*, *City of Karachi* and *City of Singapore*. They were single-screw cargo-only vessels, all built by Alexander Stephen & Sons, which was then enjoying a postwar boom in its order book. As for many Ellerman Line ships, routes were worldwide and the *City of Bedford* could be deployed on any itinerary with the capacity to carry a few passengers. Her well-proportioned profile typified the era of the early 1950s, having a curved raked stem and a spoon stern. She gave her owners 22 years' service before being scrapped in 1972 at Valencia. This bow view, taken at Birkenhead on 1 September 1956, shows her with her derricks swung out towards the barrels on the quayside. She is displaying the 'blue peter' flag indicating that she is to sail within the hour. Note the cowling atop the funnel around her boiler flue uptake — a feature of the four sisters. *Kenneth Wightman*

CITY OF JOHANNESBURG

(11/1947) Ellerman Lines
(Managers: Ellerman &
Bucknall S.S. Co Ltd)
8,207grt; 497ft 6in (151.64m)
loa x 64ft 2in (19.56m) beam
Barclay, Curle & Co Ltd,
Glasgow
2 x Oil 2SA 4-cyl Doxford
(by builder): 9,000bhp

The *City of Johannesburg* was completed postwar for Ellerman as a one-off cargo ship with twin screws driven by Doxford diesels. The performance of this engine configuration may well have influenced the decision to use a similar plant in the later *City of Port Elizabeth* class, as she could comfortably manage 16 knots. She entered service for Ellerman & Bucknall on their UK to South and East Africa route. In addition to having a deadweight tonnage of 10,610 she could also carry 12 passengers. The blockade of Beira at the time of Unilateral Declaration of Independence (UDI) in Rhodesia may have limited her effectiveness by interfering with her scheduled itinerary. She was sold to Greek interests in 1970 and renamed *Filothei*. Two years later she was again renamed *Lyavitos*, still under the Greek flag, finally being sold for scrapping at Kaohsiung in 1973. This picture of her, taken in June 1964, shows her hove to and high in the water at an unknown location. It is perhaps not widely known that Ellerman's faster ships operated from Hull. *Kenneth Wightman*

CITY OF PORT ELIZABETH

(12/1952) Ellerman Lines
13,363grt; 541ft
    (164.90m) loa x 71ft 2in
    (21.69m) beam
Vickers-Armstrongs Ltd,
    Newcastle
2 x Oil 2SA 6-cyl Doxford
    by Hawthorn, Leslie &
    Co, Newcastle:
    12,650bhp

The *City of Port Elizabeth* was the lead ship of a class of four ships designed to make the passage from London to Cape Town in 15 days at a service speed of 16½ knots. For the time, they offered sheer luxury to the 107 first-class passengers that could be accommodated. All cabins were on A and B decks with those on A deck being fitted with private bathrooms, whilst those on B deck had shared facilities. The *City of Port Elizabeth*'s main revenue, however, was generated from the 11,400 tons of cargo she could carry. Cargo carrying capacity was 607,000cu ft in five holds, three forward and two aft. Their itinerary took them from London to Las Palmas, Cape Town, Port Elizabeth, East London, Durban, Lourenço Marques and Beira. The *City of Port Elizabeth* was launched on 12 March 1952 and sailed from London on her maiden voyage to Beira on 10 January 1953. The changing politics in Southern Africa following the Unilateral Declaration of Independence (UDI) in Rhodesia during 1965 and the implementation of the Beira Patrol operations may well have affected the quartet's prospects. She continued in this service until 1970 when, though only 18 years old, she was sold along with her three sisters to the Michael A. Karageorgis Group of Greece which planned to convert them into car ferries for the Patras to Ancona route. Renamed *Mediterranean Island* in 1971 she remained idle, however, and her planned conversion, like that of former sister *Mediterranean Dolphin* ex-*City of Durban*, did not materialise. Nor did a later concept for their adaptation into luxury cruise ships and they remained laid up instead. Despite this, the former *City of Port Elizabeth* was again renamed in 1975, becoming the *Mediterranean Sun*. As a point of interest her other former sisters, *City of Exeter* and *City of York*, did complete the transformation. After a period of further idleness she was sold in 1980 for demolition by Long Jong Industry Co, Kaohsiung, Taiwan. The picture was taken in February 1967 while the *City of Port Elizabeth* was berthed in London's Royal Albert Dock, surrounded by lighters. *Kenneth Wightman*

ESSEX

(5/1954) Federal Steam
   Navigation Co
10,936grt; 525ft 10in
   (160.27m) loa x 70ft 2in
   (21.38m) beam
John Brown & Co Ltd,
   Clydebank
2 x Oil 2SA 12-cyl Sulzer
   (by builder): 11,500bhp

Following her launch on 21 December 1953, the *Essex* scraped along the side of P&O's *Arcadia*, which was then being fitted out at John Brown's yard. It was an inauspicious start but, fortunately, only superficial damage was caused. Her sister ship was the New Zealand Shipping Co's cadet ship *Otaki*. The twin Sulzer diesel engines of the *Essex* were single reduction geared with electro-magnetic slip couplings to a single shaft, an arrangement that only found limited application. She had a refrigerated cargo capacity of 476,000cu ft and a general cargo capacity of 189,000cu ft and, with the exception of her four cadets and 12 boys, she had single cabins for the entire 71-man crew. In April 1956, she created a record — subsequently broken — by being the largest Conference cargo liner to negotiate the Victoria Channel to Dunedin. In October 1971 she was switched to P&O's General Cargo Division but retained her Federal Line livery. Two years later, during April 1973 she was transferred to P&O ownership and colours only to be disposed of in December 1975 when she was sold to Guan Guan Shipping (Pte) Ltd of Singapore and renamed *Golden Gulf*. After a further 15 months of service for these owners, during which the more efficient containerisation method of cargo-handling continued to proliferate, she was sold for demolition and arrived at Gadani Beach, Karachi on 13 March 1977 for scrapping. Taken in August 1964, the picture shows the *Essex* turning in the River Thames, assisted by a Gamecock tug. *Kenneth Wightman*

NORFOLK

(12/1936) ex *Essex* (1947) ex
  Paringa (1955) Federal
  Steam Navigation Co
  (Managers: New Zealand
  Shipping Co)
11,080grt; 551ft 3in
  (168.02m) loa x 70ft 5in
  (21.46m) beam
John Brown & Co Ltd,
  Clydebank
2 x Oil 2SA 5-cyl Doxford
  (by builder)

This ship had a chequered career following her completion in December 1936 as the *Essex* for the P&O Line. Two sister-ships, the *Sussex* (1937) and *Suffolk* (1939), followed her. All three were operated as Federal Line ships, the first two wholly owned by P&O on whose postwar Australian service they all later ran. During January 1941 the *Essex* was switched to the dangerous Malta convoy run. It was whilst at Valletta, on 16th of that month, that she was bombed in an air raid with the loss of 17 lives, also sustaining extensive structural damage. Towed to Frenchman's Creek where she was further damaged in a raid on 7 March 1941, she remained laid up there until August 1943 when she commenced a perilous voyage under tow, back to Falmouth for repairs. These took 11 months to complete. Subsequently, she was transferred to P&O's service to Australia and New Zealand in February 1947 and renamed *Paringa*. As such she was painted in their black and ochre cargo livery. In 1955 she was transferred to New Zealand Shipping Co management and renamed *Norfolk* as a unit of the Federal Line fleet. Seven years later, in July 1962, she was sold to Japanese shipbreakers for £130,000 and left New Plymouth for Yokosuka that August. This clear but undated photograph of the *Norfolk* in the Liverpool Docks highlights her age, exemplified by her straight stem. The Federal Line practice of having the crew accommodation located entirely amidships, as it was on the *Norfolk*, was well in advance of the usual standard of the day. *Kenneth Wightman*

NOTTINGHAM
(6/1950) Federal Steam
  Navigation Co
6,689grt; 480ft 4in
  (146.61m) loa x 61ft 8in
  (18.80m) beam
John Brown & Co Ltd,
  Clydebank
Oil 2SA 6-cyl Doxford by
  John Brown: 6,200bhp

When she entered service, the *Nottingham* was the smallest ship in the combined Federal Line/New Zealand Shipping Co fleets, intended for the Australian service. She had a refrigerated cargo capacity of 288,760cu ft and general cargo capacity of 196,840cu ft. In July 1958 she was one of some 130 ships chartered through the Baltic Exchange to the People's Republic of China to carry out two round voyages between Chinese ports, including Shanghai, Hong Kong and major European ports. The *Nottingham* remained on charter for about a year before returning to her normal duties on the Australian route. Possibly affected by the impending decision by the UK to join the European Common Market, with its inevitable impact on Commonwealth trade, she was sold for demolition after only 21years in service and was scrapped in Taiwan in 1971. In this view, the *Nottingham* is seen arriving off the Tilbury Landing Stage in August 1966. From the appearance of her smoke she is probably firing up her Donkey boiler prior to docking. A Soviet liner of the *Mikhail Kalinin* class is docked beyond her stern, to the right of the picture. *Kenneth Wightman*

OTAIO

(4/1958) Federal Steam Navigation Co

13,314grt; 526ft 2in (160.38m) loa x 73ft 3in (22.33m) beam

John Brown & Co Ltd, Clydebank

2 x Oil 2SA 6-cyl Doxford (by builder): 12,400bhp

The *Otaio* was completed at a cost of £2,750,000 as a purpose-built cargo ship for the New Zealand Shipping Co to be manned by cadets. As the MoT Alternative Training Scheme for Marine Engineers had been introduced in 1951, she was arranged to carry 30 engineering cadets, in addition to her 40 deck cadets, with fully fitted-out classrooms, a workshop and laboratory aboard. The trainees spent two years on the *Otaio* before being transferred to other ships in the Federal Line/New Zealand Shipping Co fleet for 18 months sea time. Their final year of training was spent ashore. The string of portholes along her port-side main deck may give a clue to the extra classrooms and workshops that were fitted into her for her training ship role. Apart from her cadet ship role, the *Otaio* was also a full working cargo ship with a refrigerated cargo capacity of 429,300cu ft. On 1 January 1966 her funnel was painted in Federal livery and exactly a year later she transferred fully to Federal Line ownership. From October 1971 she became part of P&O's General cargo Division before passing into P&O's ownership 18 months later, on 19 April 1973. On 21 July 1976 she was sold to Laggan Bay Shipping Co of Liberia and renamed *Eastern Academy,* still retaining her role as a training ship. During 1981 she was sold again, to the Arabian Maritime Transport Co of Saudi Arabia, and later in the following year, on 11 October 1982, she was sold for scrap at Gadani Beach, Karachi. The photograph shows the *Otaio* in Federal Line livery, taken in November 1968. She probably showed a good return on her investment, being manned by cadets on trainees' pay rates, whose development as professional personnel was of direct benefit to the company. *Mick Lindsay*

GEESTBAY

(7/1964) Geest Line
7,891grt; 488ft 3in
(148.82m) loa x 61ft 9in
(18.82m) beam
Nederland Dok & Schps,
Amsterdam
Oil 2SA 7-cyl Sulzer by
N. V. Werkspoor,
Amsterdam: 10,500bhp

To establish their expansion into the UK, the Dutch-owned holding company had ordered two similar ships, built in the Netherlands, the *Geestbay* and *Geestport*. They were fast cargo liners capable of carrying 200,000 stems of bananas. The *Geestbay* provided a direct service to Barbados and the Windward Islands with regular sailings from Barry in South Wales. General cargo and 12 passengers were carried on the outward journey. The *Geestbay* had five insulated holds with a total capacity of 321,436cu ft. Her all-welded hull had a raked bulbous bow and what was referred to as a 'clear water' stern, without any bilge keels. Rolling of the ship in a heavy seaway was damped by the Flume stabilisation system (based on water ballast being moved from one side of the ship to the other in a baffled athwartships tank). By using this system her banana cargo would not suffer damage during a rough Atlantic crossing. The *Geestbay* was sold in 1972 to K/S A/S Noja Ltd, Norway and renamed *North Star*. Three years later she was acquired by the Liberian concern Maritime Company Overseas Inc for whom she operated as the *Isla Verde*. This picture of the *Geestbay* shows her berthed alongside the New Fresh Wharf Limited in the Pool of London in August 1964. It clearly shows her continental design, futuristic for the 1960s, which would become the basis for future Geest Line ships. She is dressed overall, possibly on the occasion of her maiden voyage and inauguration of the new service. The *Geestbay* was one of very few British cargo liners to be registered at Boston, Lincs. *Kenneth Wightman*

CARDIGANSHIRE

(10/1950) ex *Bellerophon* (1957) Glen
  (Shire) Line
7,724grt; 487ft (148.43m) loa x 62ft
  4in (19.00m) beam
Caledon S. B. & Eng. Co Ltd, Dundee
Oil 2SA 7-cyl Burmeister & Wain by
  J. G. Kinkaid & Co, Greenock:
  7,600bhp

Constructed for Blue Funnel as the *Bellerophon*, the first of the 'A' class Mk III variants, after seven seasons this typically British-styled refrigerated cargo liner joined Glen's Shire Line as the *Cardiganshire*. She reverted to the name *Bellerophon* in 1972 on her return to Blue Funnel. However, she was then registered with the China Mutual Steam Navigation Co rather than with the Ocean Steamship Co, her original Blue Funnel group owners. In 1975 she was transferred to Elder Dempster without change of name but within months was sold to Saudi-Europe Line Ltd as the *Obhor*. Three years later, in 1978, she was chartered by a movie production company for the making of the film 'The Sailor Who Fell Out of Grace with the Sea', temporarily renamed *Belle*. Thereafter, she was broken up at Gadani Beach, Karachi from that September. *Mick Lindsay*

GLENARTNEY
(1940) Glen Line
8,986grt; 507ft (154.52m) loa
  x 66ft 5in (20.24m) beam
Caledon S.B. & Eng. Co Ltd,
  Dundee
2 x Oil 2DA 6-cyl by
  Burmeister & Wain,
  Copenhagen

Completed during wartime, the refrigerated cargo ship *Glenartney* initially featured a shortened funnel and masts, with a dummy pole mast deliberately placed off-centre to her port side as an artifice to confuse U-boat commanders while taking bearings. Employed at first in a commercial capacity, despite being painted grey, she later served as a fast supply ship from 1941. The *Glenartney* took part in the Malta relief convoy 'Operation Portcullis' in the following December, later in the war transferring to the Pacific Fleet where she demonstrated her valuable logistical capabilities in exercises transferring stores at sea at high speed. She resumed commercial service on the Far East run in 1946 continuing in this capacity until 1967 when she was sold for scrapping at Onomichi, Japan, making her final voyage to the breakers from Kobe. The *Glenartney* is depicted berthed in the King George V Dock with, beyond her, P&O's *Chusan* and one of Cunard Line's *Saxonia* class. *Kenneth Wightman*

RADNORSHIRE

(1/1948) ex *Achilles* (1949) Glen (Shire) Line
7,632grt; 487ft (148.43m) loa x 62ft 4in (19.00m) beam
Caledon S. B. & Eng. Co Ltd, Dundee
Oil 2DA 8-cyl Burmeister & Wain by J.G. Kinkaid & Co,
   Greenock: 6,800bhp

Operated by the Glen (Shire) Line from April 1949, the *Radnorshire*, seen off the King George V Dock in this striking bow-on shot, was built as the *Achilles* for the Ocean Steamship Co (Blue Funnel). She was the sixth unit of the 'A' class Mk I ships. After 13 years working the Shire Line's Far East service out of London, she returned to her former owners in December 1962, allocated the name *Asphalion*. In January 1966 she moved to Holt's Dutch subsidiary NSM 'Ocean' as the *Polyphemus*, transferring back to Blue Funnel in November 1972, assuming the name *Asphalion* for the second time. Three years later, in October 1975, she was sold to Gulf (Shipowners) Ltd, London and renamed *Gulf Anchor*. She was broken up at Kaohsiung in 1979. Note the man energetically rowing a dinghy in the foreground —a rather dangerous manoeuvre between ship and quay to take the painter for one of the *Radnorshire*'s bow lines. *Kenneth Wightman*

DEFENDER
(10/1955) T. & J. Harrison (Charente Steamship Co Ltd)
8,367grt; 464ft 9in (141.65m) loa x 59ft 5in (18.11m) beam
William Doxford & Sons Ltd, Sunderland
Oil 2SA 4-cyl (by builder): 4,800bhp

Harrisons built up their depleted fleet immediately after the end
of World War 2 using emergency-built tonnage. A number of US
'Liberty' ships were purchased, as well as British-built 'Empire'
vessels. In addition a vigorous newbuilding programme was
undertaken. The company's first motor ship was the *Herdsman* of
1947 soon to be followed by a growing fleet of motor vessels,
many delivered by the preferred builder of the day, William
Doxford & Sons of Sunderland. By 1955 the *Defender* had joined

the fleet as a general cargo ship fitted with a heavy lift derrick fore and aft, and capable of a speed of 13 knots. She remained with the company
until 1975 when she was sold for further trading to Polimars Marine Corp, Panama as the *Euromariner*. Two years later, from September 1977,
she was broken up at Cartagena, Colombia. In this undated view she is seen in the River Clyde in company with vessels of the Clyde Shipping
Company. Her Harrison Line funnel colours, referred to as 'two of fat and one of lean' can be readily seen. *Mick Lindsay*

ROYSTON GRANGE
(12/1959) Houlder line
10,262grt; 489ft (149.04m) loa x 65ft 8in (20.01m) beam
Hawthorn Leslie (Shipbuilders) Ltd, Newcastle
2 x double-reduction geared steam turbines (by builder): 8,500shp

Houlder Brothers' refrigerated ship *Royston Grange*, sister to the
Denby Grange and *Hardwicke Grange*, was the victim of one of the
most harrowing disasters to befall a cargo vessel on the British
Register. Thirteen years after she entered service, on 11 May 1972,
she collided in dense fog with a Liberian tanker, the *Tien Chee*, in
the River Plate, off Montevideo. Loaded with frozen and chilled
meat and butter, and carrying 10 passengers, the *Royston Grange*
had just sailed from Buenos Aires. Resulting from the collision, a
fire ignited aboard the British ship engulfing it so rapidly that there
was no means or opportunity for those aboard her to escape. Her
entire 63-man crew, all the passengers and the Argentine river pilot,

who was still on board, were killed. The accident occurred just two miles from the site of the wreck of the scuttled German pocket battleship
Admiral Graf Spee. The gutted hulk of the *Royston Grange*, declared a constructive total loss, was subsequently towed to Barcelona for breaking
up. The photograph shows her in better times, berthed in London's Royal Victoria Dock. *Kenneth Wightman*

WESTBURY

(11/1960) Alexander Shipping Co Ltd
 (Houlder Bros)
8,533grt; 457 ft (139.29m) loa x 62ft
 (18.90m) beam
Burntisland Shipbuilding Co Ltd,
 Burntisland
Oil 2SA 5-cyl Doxford by Hawthorn,
 Leslie (Eng) Ltd, Newcastle: 5,500bhp

The *Westbury* was built for the Alexander Shipping Line and was a sister ship to the *Shaftsbury,* but both were managed by Houlder Brothers and sported Houlder Line livery. She was a general cargo ship of 11,900 tons deadweight, with a speed of 13½ knots. Her Doxford engines were of the opposed-piston type. In 1975 she transferred under the Furness Withy holding group to Shaw Savill & Albion and again two years later to the Welldeck Shipping Co. In 1978 she was sold to National Glory Cia. Nav. SA, Greece and renamed *Diamondo* and then resold to another Greek company, Iktinos Shipping Co, in 1981 and renamed *Polana*. She was only in service with them for two years, being scrapped at Gadani Beach, Karachi from May 1983. The photograph shows the *Westbury* alongside, possibly at Liverpool, discharging cargo with her own derricks. *Mick Lindsay*

JAMAICA PLANTER

(12/1959) Jamaica Banana
  Producers
6,159grt; 445ft 7in
  (135.81m) loa x 56ft 6in
  (17.22m) beam
Lithgows Ltd, Port
  Glasgow
2 x double-reduction
  geared steam turbines
  by D. Rowan & Co,
  Glasgow: 8,750bhp

A regular visitor to the King George V Dock, the *Jamaica Planter* was specially designed for service between the West Indies and the UK for the carriage of 1,900 tons of bananas, plus other fruits like mangoes and pawpaws. In consort with the 1934-built *Jamaica Producer* — herself replaced by a new ship of the same name in 1962 — she operated in direct competition with the ships of Fyffes and the United Fruit Company. Characterised by a modern, continental design, she could accommodate 12 passengers in attractively furnished cabins. Launched on 10 August 1959, the refrigerated cargo vessel *Jamaica Planter* entered the fruit trade between Kingston, Jamaica and London that December, maintaining a service speed of 17 knots although during trials she had attained a mean speed of just over 19 knots. After 14 years service with her original owners, she was sold in 1974 to Universal Seaways Co Private Ltd of Singapore and renamed *Fine Fruit*. Two years later, after an extremely short career, she was sold for breaking up at Kaohsiung, Taiwan. No doubt, her steam turbines had proved expensive to operate at a time of rapidly increasing fuel costs. The photograph, thought to have been taken in the Royal Group of Docks in February 1973 just prior to her sale out of the Jamaica Banana Producers Association fleet, shows her ready to discharge her cargo. By then some 14 years old, her attractive lines reveal a design well ahead of its time. *Mick Lindsay*

JAMAICA PRODUCER

(6/1934) Jamaica Banana Producers
5,598grt; 423ft (128.92m) loa x 54ft
9in (16.69m) beam
Lithgows Ltd, Port Glasgow
Quadruple expansion 4-cyl steam
reciprocating by D. Rowan & Co,
Glasgow

One of three similar ships constructed for the service from Kingston to London, the *Jamaica Producer* and her sisters, *Jamaica Progress* and *Jamaica Pioneer*, combined a large refrigerated storage space, of 260,000cu ft, for banana cargoes, with berths for 12 passengers. Her consorts were both war losses, sunk in July and August 1940 respectively. The *Jamaica Producer* herself had a close scrape when attacked by a Heinkel aircraft in August 1941. But the aircraft approached so low in its attack run that it clipped her foremast sending it plummeting into the sea and allowing the *Jamaica Producer* to escape. This close-up view shows the ship's midship details, revealing the style, construction and deck equipment of a vessel of her vintage. The *Jamaica Producer* was replaced by another vessel of the same name completed in June 1962. *Kenneth Wightman*

BELLOC
(2/1980) Lamport & Holt
9,324grt; 472ft 5in
   (144.0m) loa x 67ft 1in
   (20.45m) beam
Austin & Pickersgill Ltd,
   Southwick, Sunderland
Oil 2SA 4-cyl Sulzer by
   G. Clarke N.E.M:
   17,650bhp

Viewed at London, on 13 September 1981, the *Belloc* is an example of the SD14 design, a shelter deck type introduced in 1967 as a Liberty ship replacement. Within 10 years, more than 150 of these standard vessels had been built, the majority at the Sunderland yard of Austin & Pickersgill. Others were built under licence in Greece, Brazil and Argentina and in other British shipyards. The *Belloc* was managed by Lamport & Holt for the Belloc Shipping Co, reflecting a ship management practice — the creation of single-ship subsidiaries — which became increasingly popular from the 1960s, no doubt for tax advantages. Lamport & Holt had themselves been acquired by the Vestey Group in June 1944, in association with Frederick Leyland & Co Ltd, itself purchased in 1935. In 1981, barely a year after her delivery, the *Belloc* was sold to Yugoslav-flag owners Montenegro Overseas Nav. Ltd under the name *Piva*. Eleven years later, she moved on to Bar Overseas Shipping Co Ltd, under the Maltese flag, renamed *Rio B*. The next move, in 1997, saw her transferred to other Maltese owners, Domino Shipping Co Ltd, and then in 2000 she was sold again when, as the *Pangani*, she joined the Singapore owners, Yong Shun Shipping Private Ltd. She was still registered with this concern in May 2004. Numerous SD14 design derivatives were constructed, such that the type could hardly be described as 'standard', but, ultimately, the trend to containerisation reduced the demand for this type of vessel. *Mick Lindsay*

RONSARD
(9/1957) Lamport & Holt
7,840grt; 472ft 8in (144.01m)
  loa x 62ft (18.37m) beam
Bartram & Sons Ltd,
  Sunderland
Oil 2SA 6-cyl Doxford by
  N.E. Marine Eng. Co,
  Wallsend-on-Tyne:
  7,500bhp

After its brief flirtation with steam turbine propulsion, Lamport & Holt returned to the motor ship once more with the *Raphael* of 1953 and the Sunderland-built *Ronsard*. The *Ronsard* was initially completed for the Salient Shipping Co Ltd of Bermuda which, to all intents and purposes, came under the Vestey interests along with Blue Star and Booth Line. She was immediately hired on bareboat charter to Lamport & Holt. Three years later, in 1960, she was transferred to that company's ownership. The *Ronsard* and her sisters were designed to transit the Manchester Ship Canal. To permit this, their forward topmast was made from wood and could be lowered.

This was done in conjunction with ballasting of the ship by the head, lowering her in the water. During 1980 she was sold to Obestain Inc of Panama and renamed *Obestain*. A year later on 8 August 1981 she sailed on her last voyage from Bangkok for Taiwan where she was scrapped at Kaohsiung. In this photograph taken in March 1973, the *Ronsard* is seen berthed at Cardiff. *Mick Lindsay*

CAPE HORN
(6/1957) Lyle Shipping
8,484grt; 478ft 6in (145.84m) loa x
    60ft 3in (18.37m) beam
Lithgows Ltd, Port Glasgow
Oil 2SA 5-cyl Burmeister & Wain by
    J.G. Kinkaid & Co, Greenock:
    4,500bhp

Launched on 27 February 1957 for the Lyle Shipping Company of Glasgow, the *Cape Horn* entered service that summer, working her owners' routes to the Mediterranean. The photograph shows her during a call at Gibraltar. The effect of changing trades led to her early redundancy in the Lyle fleet and she was sold in 1967 to South Shipping Co Ltd, Gibraltar and renamed *South Venture*. Under this name, she met her end on 22 October 1972. While on voyage from Cartagena, Colombia to Puerto Barrios, Guatemala in ballast, she ran aground on Roncador Cay, in the Caribbean Sea, at position latitude 13°29'N, longitude 80°02'W. Leaking throughout, it was impossible to refloat her and the wreck was abandoned as a constructive total loss. Salvage tugs picked up her crew and took them to Cristobal.
Mick Lindsay

ASSIOUT

(10/1949) Moss Hutchison Line

3,422grt; 366ft 11in (111.84m) loa x 52ft 2in
(15.90m) beam

Harland & Wolff Ltd, Belfast

Oil 4SA 8-cyl Burmeister & Wain (by
builder): 3,500bhp

A smallish cargo ship by comparison with others of the day built for the Liverpool to Mediterranean run and Liverpool to west coast of France and Spain service, operated out of the Alexandria Branch Dock, Liverpool. Following a lengthy service with Moss Hutchison the *Assiout* was absorbed into P&O's General Cargo Division on 1 October 1971. Later on 3 March 1973 she was sold to Apollonianov Shipping Co SA of Greece and renamed *Chryssoulah II*. She was sold during 1981 to Admiral Ltd of Pakistan and arrived at Gadani Beach, Karachi on 19 November 1981 where demolition commenced a month later. The picture, dated February 1972, shows the *Assiout* berthed at an unknown location. *Mick Lindsay*

TABOR

(3/1952) Moss Hutchison Line
3,694grt; 385ft 4in (117.45m) loa x 55ft 2in (16.81m)
  beam
Caledon S. B. & E. Co Ltd, Dundee
Oil 2SA 4-cyl Doxford by Hawthorn, Leslie & Co,
  Newcastle: 4,450bhp

The *Tabor* joined Moss Hutchison's all-motorship
company in March 1952 and with a speed of 14½ knots
was the fastest cargo ship to join the company up until
then. Moss Hutchinson carried on its continental
operations until P&O General Cargo Division were
appointed its managers and its fleet was absorbed.
The *Tabor* came under the control of the new Division on
1 October 1971 and was later registered in the ownership
of P&O on 18 April 1973. After two and a half years of
trading with them she was sold to Apollonianov Shipping
Co SA of Greece and renamed *Katia*. During 1982 she
was sold to Kate Shipping Co Ltd of Malta and named *Kate*. That same year she was sold on to Steel Industries Kerala Ltd, India for demolition.
She arrived at Beypore, India on 11 March 1982 for scrapping. The photograph shows the *Tabor* berthed alongside at Cardiff during March 1969.
Mick Lindsay

ARDFINNAN

(1/1945) ex *Validemosa* (1961) ex *Sheaf Mount* (1957)
  ex *Empire Fancy* (1947) Mullion & Co, Hong Kong —
  British Registry
7,133grt; 443ft 1in (135.05m) loa x 57ft (17.37m) beam
Burntisland S. B. Co Ltd, Burntisland
Oil 2SA 3-cyl by William Doxford & Sons, Sunderland

A typical tramp steamer from the immediate postwar
period, the *Ardfinnan* was photographed off Hong Kong
in April 1965. Three years later she was transferred to a
sister company, Mullion & Co, Gibraltar and renamed
Court Harwell. As such, on 9 September 1968 during
typhoon 'Wendy', she was driven ashore at Haiphong,
Vietnam. Though refloated seven days later, her days were
numbered and in the following June she went to Hong
Kong to be broken up by Ming Hing & Co. *Mick Lindsay*

COROMANDEL

(10/1949) P&O Steam Navigation Co
7,065grt; 484ft 5in (147.65m) loa x 62ft
   11in (19.18m) beam
Barclay, Curle & Co, Glasgow
Oil 2SA 6-cyl Doxford (by builder):
   6,800bhp

Along with her sister the *Cannanore*, the *Coromandel* entered a postwar fleet of steamships, and was initially operated as a general cargo liner with a capacity for 545,758cu ft and an insulated capacity of 20,694cu ft. She was launched on 20 December 1948 and operated on P&O's Europe to India and later their Far Eastern services. In November 1969 she was sold to Jebshun Shipping of Hong Kong and renamed *Shun Hing*. On 25 June 1972 she was driven ashore at Manila by typhoon 'Konsing'. The following year she was twice sold and renamed *Hop Sing* before arriving at Kaohsiung for demolition on 14 April 1973. The photograph shows a good broadside view of the *Coromandel*, a typical improved postwar design that eventually emerged from the wartime emergency ships. Her deckhouse aft was the accommodation for the Lascar (East Indian) crew that was carried by all P&O vessels. *Mick Lindsay*

DEVANHA
(1/1947) ex *Lautoka* (1947) ex
   Tarbatness (1947) P&O Steam
   Navigation Co
7,375grt; 441ft 5in (134.54m) loa x 57ft
   2in (17.42m) beam
West Coast Shipbuilding Ltd, Vancouver
Triple expansion 3-cyl steam
   reciprocating by Dominion
   Engineering Works, Latching, Quebec:
   2,250 ihp

On 29 May 1945, just after World War 2 ended in Europe, the Canadian yard had completed the Admiralty maintenance ship *Tarbatness* too late for its intended role. Lautoka Steamship Ltd of Fiji bought the ship and converted her and she entered service as the *Lautoka* in January 1947. Nine months later she was bought by P&O and renamed *Devanha*. She had a capacity of 479,754cu ft and was employed on P&O's Australia to India and later UK to India/Pakistan services. Although she was a reliable vessel to operate, her triple expansion steam engines could only manage a top speed of 10½ knots and that made her a lot slower than her P&O consorts. Hence, she was sold on 11 April 1961 to Fraternity Shipping Co of Hong Kong and renamed *Fortune Canary*. This was followed in 1964 by sale to another Hong Kong concern, Hai An Shipping Co, under the name, *Wing An*. In 1972 she was sold to Hardware Manufacturing Corp. of Pakistan for demolition and she arrived at Karachi on 24 January 1972 for scrapping. This shot shows her in a fully laden condition, arriving off Thameshaven. No doubt as a result of carrying Lascars in her crew, she appears, by her gleaming upperworks, to be well maintained. *Kenneth Wightman*

KHYBER

(1945) ex *Stanmore* (1947) ex *Mahanoy City Victory*
  (1947) P&O Steam Navigation Co
7,675grt; 455ft 4in (138.79m) loa x 62ft 1in (18.93m)
  beam
Bethlehem Fairfield Shipyard Inc, Baltimore, Maryland
2 x double-reduction geared steam turbines by
  Westinghouse Electric & Manufacturing Co,
  Pittsburgh: 6,000shp

An example of a wartime US-built cargo ship, the *Khyber* was completed as one of the emergency-built 'Victory' ships. After her launch on
24 February 1945 she entered service a month later as the *Mahanoy City Victory* for the US War Shipping Administration. After the war, she was
bought during 1947 by the Stanhope SS Co of London and renamed *Stanmore*. With a cargo capacity of 453,197cu ft and a speed of 16 knots, she
offered great potential and attracted the attention of P&O, which purchased her on 9 September of the same year and renamed her *Khyber*. She was
operated on their London-Calcutta/Far Eastern services until she was sold on 24 April 1964 to Dragon Steamship Co of Liberia and renamed *Comet
Victory*. Four years later she was sold to another Liberian company and renamed *Ocean Comet*. In 1969 she was sold to Yung Tai Steel & Iron works
of Taiwan and arrived for scrapping at Kaohsiung in January 1970. The picture shows the *Khyber* off Tilbury in April 1963 with a Gamecock tug
alongside. The view clearly captures her wartime profile just a year before she was sold out of the company. *Kenneth Wightman*

PATONGA

(12/1953) P&O Steam Navigation Co
10,071grt; 499ft 8in (152.30m) loa x 64ft 8in (19.71m)
  beam
Alexander Stephen & Sons, Linthouse, Glasgow
3 x double-reduction geared steam turbines (by builder):
  8,000shp

Another of P&O's general cargo liners, with a capacity
of 379,212cu ft making it the largest cargo vessel to
enter their service up until the mid-1960s, the *Patonga*
was launched on 11 August 1953. She was employed on
P&O's UK-Australia cargo service. On 1 October 1971
she transferred to P&O's General Cargo Division and as
such her funnel was eventually repainted from the
traditional black colour to a corporate light blue shade
adorned with the letters P&O in white drop-shadow
style. On 28 May 1975 she was renamed *Strathlauder* but her time with the new name was short-lived and she arrived at Karachi on 19 September
1977 and four days later was sold to Pakistan Management Corp Ltd for scrap. This picture of the *Patonga* was taken in May 1973, possibly off
Gravesend, and shows her looking rather shabby prior to receiving the new colours described above. Note the flue extension protruding from the
funnel top, which was fitted some time after building. *Mick Lindsay*

SURAT

(10/1948) P&O Steam Navigation Co

8,925grt; 522ft (159.11m) loa x 67ft 3in (20.50m) beam

Vickers-Armstrongs Naval Yard, Walker-on-Tyne, Newcastle

3 x steam turbines, 1 each double-reduction geared HP and single-reduction geared IP and LP, by Vickers-Armstrongs, Barrow-in-Furness: 13,000shp

Launched on 28 November 1947, only a month later than the *Soudan*, the *Surat* could be considered as a half-sister to the *Soudan* and *Somali,* being of a similar length, gross and deadweight tonnage but having steam, rather than diesel propulsion. She entered P&O's Far Eastern service, enjoying an incident-free career until 23 January 1964 when, during a voyage from Kushiro to Yokohama in Japan, she ran aground and sustained serious bottom damage to her hull that required major repairs. On 10 September 1968 she was renamed *Pando Head*. Three years later, on 1 October 1971, she was transferred to P&O's General Cargo Division for which she served another six months before being sold to T. W. Ward Ltd for demolition. She arrived at Inverkeithing on 15 May 1972 for scrapping to commence. The picture shows the *Surat* early in her career steaming at full speed. *Mick Lindsay*

POTOSI

(5/1955) Pacific Steam Navigation
 Co
8,564grt; 512ft 6in (156.21m) loa
 x 66ft 3in (20.19m) beam
Greenock Dockyard Co Ltd,
 Greenock
3 x double-reduction geared steam
 turbines by Marine Turbine Co,
 Wallsend-on-Tyne: 10,340shp

Built as a sister ship to the *Pizarro*, the *Potosi* was the fourth Pacific Steam Navigation ship to bear the name. She was launched on 23 February 1955 and completed that year for the company's arduous service between Liverpool and the west coast of South America via the Panama Canal and sometimes returning through the Straits of Magellan. Like the *Pizarro* she could manage an average speed of 16 knots, very creditable for its day but a growing number of more economical motor ships were being built for the long-haul voyage to South America. Thus, the *Potosi* served Pacific Steam Navigation for only 17 years before being sold in 1972 to Granvias Oceanicos Armadora SA of Piraeus and renamed *Kavo Peiratis*. After another four years she was sold to W. H. Arnott Young & Co, during October 1976, for demolition at Dalmuir — a premature ending for a reliable and safe vessel. The picture shows the *Potosi* berthed in the Mersey Docks with Elder Dempster's *Apapa* to her stern. Although not dated, the photograph is thought to date from around 1957 or 1958. Note her high sheer, designed to take the Pacific swell when steaming down the west coast of South America.
Kenneth Wightman

SANTANDER

(5/1946) Pacific Steam Navigation Co
8,550grt; 466ft 4in (142.14m) loa x 62ft 10in
   (19.15m) beam
Harland & Wolff, Belfast
Oil 2DA 8-cyl (by builder): 7,500bhp

The *Santander* and her sister, the *Salinas* of 1947, were postwar additions to Pacific Steam's fleet and with their single double-acting H&W diesel engine were ideally suited to the long voyage to South America. Relatively small in comparison with Royal Mail's vessels that operated on the East coast, they could nevertheless manage an average speed of 15½ knots. The *Santander* was sold in 1967 for £147,500 to Navmachos Steam Ship Co of Famagusta in Cyprus and renamed *Navmachos*. On 9 December 1971 she was sold for $166,000 for breaking up in Spain by Villaneuva y Geltru. The photograph shows the *Santander* underway on the River Thames in May 1966. *Kenneth Wightman*

BAMENDA PALM
(3/1956) Palm Line
5,154grt; 446ft 9in
   (136.17m) loa x 58ft 3in
   (17.75m) beam
Swan Hunter & Wigham
   Richardson Ltd,
   Newcastle
Oil 2SA 4-cyl Doxford
   (by builder): 4,500bhp

The Palm Line was originally founded in 1912 by Lever Brothers of Port Sunlight on the Wirral. Palm Line ships had carried 1½ million tons of cargo back in 1949 but by 1953 this had increased by some 10%. In order to meet this increase in trade the *Bamenda Palm* and her sister the *Badagry Palm* were added to an expanding fleet. In fact, the *Bamenda Palm* was the first of a 12-ship (six pairs) series of ships built for the company by Swan Hunter in this period. She was typical of the general cargo ships operated by the company that brought back to the UK palm oil, cocoa, groundnuts, timber and plywood from West Africa. At many of the ports along the African coast the *Bamenda Palm* would have to use her own derricks to load and discharge cargo into or from surf-boats. In 1972 she was sold to Spetsai Shipping Co Ltd of Limassol (J.G.Goumas and Co SA., Piraeus) and then transferred to another Cypriot associate, Marlinea Armadora SA Panama, under the Greek flag and renamed *Lenio*. She was sold again in 1978, to Allouette Shipping Corporation, of Piraeus and renamed *Elsa S.K.* A third sale in the same year took her to Associated Moineau Cia. Nav. SA of Piraeus who renamed her *Eternal Sea*. She was sold to Pakistani breakers in 1983. The photograph shows the *Bamenda Palm* docking at Southampton's Western docks. To the left of her bows and already berthed may be seen Holland America's *Nieuw Amsterdam*. *Mick Lindsay*

PORT AUCKLAND
(4/1949) Port Line
11,942grt; 559ft 9in
(170.61m) loa x 70ft 3in
(21.41m) beam
Hawthorn, Leslie & Co
Ltd, Newcastle
2 x Oil 2SA 6-cyl Doxford
(by builder): 13,200bhp

When the *Port Auckland* sailed on her maiden voyage on 19 May 1949 to New Zealand she aroused considerable interest at each port. Some observers were quick to criticise her ultra-modern design akin to some continental cargo ships of the time but postwar naval architecture was innovative enough to incorporate aesthetics with function — a bold step for the day! An unusual feature at the time was a large deck crane on her aft deck, which could handle cargo for two holds from both sides of the ship. The crane's slewing gear was so arranged that it could revolve through 360°. In 1976 she was converted into a sheep carrier by Kepple Shipyards of Singapore for Gulf Fisheries WLL of Kuwait. She was renamed *Mashaallah* and used for carrying live sheep from Australia to the Middle East but in this role she was plagued by engine problems and in 1979 she was sold to Chien Cheng Iron & Steel at Kaohsiung for scrap, arriving there on 25 October 1979. This photograph of the *Port Auckland* was probably taken at Southampton during the early 1970s. It shows that, even when rust-streaked, she was a striking vessel with a design that was still well ahead of its time. *Mick Lindsay*

PORT BRISBANE
(2/1949) Port Line
11,945grt; 559ft 11in
 (170.66m) loa x 70ft 3in
 (21.41m) beam
Swan Hunter & Wigham
 Richardson Ltd, Newcastle
2 x Oil 2SA 6-cyl Doxford by
 Wallsend Slipway Co,
 Wallsend-on-Tyne:
 13,200bhp

The *Port Brisbane,* sister to the *Port Auckland*, was ordered as Port Line's new postwar flagship. She sailed on her maiden voyage to Australia on 23 March 1949, sporting the new streamlined look with long forecastle, single mast, rounded superstructure and squat, sloping funnel. Both she and the *Port Auckland* were provided with large refrigerated capacities of 563,000cu ft, and were unique in that they were the first ships to have their holds entirely sheathed with aluminium alloy sheets. This gave a considerably weight-saving benefit of about 260 tons. Furthermore, the aluminium was cleaner and more durable than wood, which was customarily used. On 10 March 1968 the *Port Brisbane* was transferred to Blueport Management and in August 1971 she came under the control of Trafalgar House Investments. Four years later, on 2 November 1975, she arrived at Loy Ken Shipbreaking Co of Hong Kong for demolition. The picture shows the *Port Brisbane* at Liverpool in March 1974, with her derricks ready for cargo handling. Note her spare propeller stowed on the after deck above the sleek lines of her cruiser stern. *Mick Lindsay*

PORT LYTTLETON
(3/1947) Port Line
7,413grt; 487ft 10in (148.69m) loa x 63ft 8in (19.41m) beam
Hawthorn, Leslie & Co Ltd, Newcastle
Oil 2SA 6-cyl Doxford (by builder): 6,600bhp

This one-off Port Line vessel had no sister though she was comparable to her owner's *Port Lincoln* in that she had a modified bridge front, a raised poop and a more streamlined funnel. Her Doxford oil engines were of the opposed-piston type. On her maiden voyage she carried no cargo but crossed the Atlantic and Pacific in ballast to load for the first time in New Zealand. She remained employed on the MANZ run (a circular route linking Montreal and eastern seaboard of the United States, Australia and New Zealand) between the South Pacific and North America. In December 1953 she grounded on a sandbank in St Mary's River, Florida, causing severe damage to her hull amidships and beneath No 3 hold. She was drydocked at Savannah where extensive repairs had to be carried out. From 10 March 1968 she was managed by Blueport and four years later, on 7 June 1972, she arrived at Shipbreaking Industries Ltd of Faslane to be broken up. The photograph shows the *Port Lyttleton* in a light loaded condition. Her immediate postwar, almost emergency design is in marked contrast to that of the *Port Auckland* and *Port Brisbane*. *Kenneth Wightman*

SCOTTISH PRINCE
(11/1950) ex *Albemarle* (1957) ex *Afric* (1955) Prince Line
3,364grt; 364ft (110.94m) loa x 51ft 3in (15.62m) beam
Burntisland S. B. Co Ltd, Burntisland
Oil 2SA 4-cyl Doxford by Hawthorn, Leslie & Co, Newcastle:
   3,300bhp

Although built for Prince Line, the *Scottish Prince*, sister ship of the *Egyptian Prince*, first entered service as the *Afric*, so-named for a five-year charter to Shaw Savill & Albion, managed on that company's behalf by Furness, Withy. Subsequently, at the conclusion of that charter, she was chartered again to the Pacific Steam Navigation Co as the *Albemarle*, opening a hitherto untried service between Bermuda, Caribbean ports and Panama. She finally adopted the name *Scottish Prince* in 1957, maintaining Prince Line's Mediterranean services. After 11 years fulfilling these duties, she was traded to Cypriot owners Klymnos Shipping Co and renamed *Grigorios*. Four years later ownership transferred to Milos Steamship Co, Cyprus and her name changed to *Milos*, with a further change, three years later, to *Nestor*. The former *Scottish Prince* was broken up at Gadani Beach, Pakistan from late December 1977. In this striking view, picked out by a shaft of sunlight, she is hove to off the West Pier at Gravesend on 31 January 1959, barely two years after she first adopted Prince Line colours. *Kenneth Wightman*

SYRIAN PRINCE
(12/1936) Prince Line
1,988grt; 296ft 6in (90.36m) loa x 44ft 2in
  (13.46m) beam
Furness Shipbuilding Co Ltd, Haverton
  Hill-on-Tees
Triple expansion steam reciprocating by
  Richardsons Westgarth, Hartlepool:
  1,700ihp

Photographed in the Mersey Docks, the *Syrian Prince* has the John S. Monks' 523-gross-ton *Rockville* ex *Wheatcrop* alongside. Berthed beyond her are other ships of the Furness, Withy Group with, in the distance, on the cross berth, a United Fruit Company fruit carrier. The *Syrian Prince* was one of a trio of ships, the others being the *Arabian Prince* and *Palestinian Prince*. With these sisters she maintained her owner's Mediterranean trade until 1959, 23 years of service that included war duties. The *Syrian Prince* was then acquired by P. Th. Petropoulos, Cia Maritima Med, a Beirut-based concern, to be operated under the Lebanese flag as the *Sunny Med*. Five years later, in 1964, she was sold again, to Glyfada Seafaring Corp. S.A. of Piraeus, becoming the *Dinos* for the last five years of her career. On 25 October 1969, then 33 years old, she arrived at Savona, Italy, to be broken up.
Kenneth Wightman

ATLANTIC CITY

(5/1941) Reardon Smith (Leeds Shipping Co)
5,281grt; 432ft 6in (131.83m) loa x 55ft 1in (16.79m) beam
William Doxford & Sons, Sunderland
Oil 2SA 4-cyl (by builder)

One of Sir William Reardon Smith's cargo tramping ships, the wartime-completed *Atlantic City* is seen in this view dated August 1956 high in the water, in ballast, but seemingly well maintained from her clean paintwork. Over a typical 12-month period a vessel like this would frequently be in ballast when chartered for trade and would carry single-commodity cargoes such as wheat, phosphate, wheat, salt, then wheat again, on positioning voyages. Over the course of this period she could possibly steam a distance of some 60,000 miles. After 21 years' service with Reardon Smith the *Atlantic City* was sold in 1962 to Achillet Cia Nav SA of Lebanon and renamed *Achillet*. On 25 February 1971, whilst on a voyage from Sfax, Tunisia to Madras, India, she foundered off Rocky Point, Namibia, about 300 miles north-west of Walvis Bay, in position 19°00'S, 10°19'E after she sprang leaks when her hull fractured in heavy weather. It is not widely known that Reardon Smith ran its own Nautical Training School in Wales. *Mick Lindsay*

LOCH AVON

(8/1947) Royal Mail Lines
8,617grt; 498ft 4in (151.88m) loa x 66ft 4in (20.21m) beam
Harland & Wolff, Belfast
3 x double-reduction geared steam turbines (by builder):
  11,550shp

The refrigerated steam-powered cargo liner *Loch Avon* was constructed for Royal Mail Line's North Pacific service, along with a sister, the *Loch Garth*. It is believed that the photograph, taken on 21 June 1966, shows her underway in the River Rhine in the approaches to Rotterdam. A year later the *Loch Avon* was sold to Singapore Malaysia Overseas Line and renamed *Hong Kong Observer*. In 1971 she was broken up at Taiwan, outliving her former sister by three years. An interesting, distinguishing feature of this pair of cargo liners was their long, low midships structure surmounted by the funnel at one end, a raised bridge and accommodation block at the other and, between them, two sets of derricks serving an elevated hold. *Kenneth Wightman*

ATHENIC
(7/1947) Shaw Savill & Albion
15,187grt; 560 ft (170.68m) loa x 71 ft
   (21.64m) beam
Harland & Wolff, Belfast
6 x single-reduction geared steam turbines
   (by builder): 14,000shp

Second of a series of large cargo-passenger liners introduced by Shaw Savill after World War 2, the *Athenic* is seen here at London's Royal Albert Dock on 15 March 1958. Astern of her is a small British India Line ship. The four vessels of her class were placed on the London to Australia and New Zealand route via either South Africa or Panama. Provision was made for 513,320cu ft of insulated cargo and an additional 149,100cu ft of general, non-insulated cargo. Passenger accommodation was for 85 first-class passengers but this was removed in 1965. Four years later the *Athenic* was scrapped at Kaohsiung, Taiwan. *Kenneth Wightman*

CRETIC

(5/1955) Shaw Savill & Albion
11,151grt; 512ft (156.05m) loa x 69ft (21.03m) beam
Swan, Hunter & Wigham Richardson Ltd, Wallsend-on-Tyne
2 x Oil 2SA 6-cyl by William Doxford & Sons Ltd, Sunderland: 13,200bhp

Last of the five 'C'-class ships, the *Cretic* was the only one of her group to be powered by Doxford opposed-piston diesels. She was reputed to be a quieter vessel with this form of propulsion than her sisters *Canopic*, *Carnatic*, *Cedric* and *Cymric* that were fitted with Harland & Wolff oil engines. The *Cretic* was transferred to Royal Mail Line in 1973 becoming that company's *Drina*. Four years later, she was sold to Singapore owners, Lancaster Shipping Co, for which Shaw Savill & Albion acted as managers, and renamed *United Vigour*. She continued trading for two more years, until 1979 when she was broken up in Taiwan. *Kenneth Wightman*

IONIC

(3/1959) Shaw Savill & Albion
11,219grt; 513 ft (156.35m) loa
   x 70ft (21.33m) beam
Cammell Laird & Co,
   Birkenhead
Oil 2SA 8-cyl by Harland &
   Wolff, Belfast: 11,300bhp

Lead ship of the same class of reefers as the *Illyric*, *Iberic* and *Icenic*, the *Ionic* is seen in the Thames, arriving off the Royal Docks Group. Shaw Savill's 'I' class quartet were a modified development of the earlier 'C' class, of which, for comparison, the *Cretic* is also shown here. Unlike their predecessors, they had only a single turbo-charged engine that operated on heavy oil. Although the total cargo volume of each class was comparable, it was distributed rather differently. The 'I' class had a greater capacity for chilled cargoes, some 63% of the total of 650,000cu ft, whereas on the 'C' class it was split almost 50:50 between insulated and general cargo. This was perhaps an indication of the cargo that was most valuable to Shaw Savill. The *Ionic* was traded to Panorea Shipping Co, Cyprus, in 1978, taking the new name *Glenparva*. She continued operating for another year but was then sold for breaking up. *Kenneth Wightman*

MEDIC

(7/1963) Shaw Savill & Albion
12,220grt; 538ft (163.97m) loa x 71ft (21.64m) beam
Swan, Hunter & Wigham Richardson Ltd, Newcastle-on-
Tyne
Oil 2SA 7-cyl by Harland & Wolff, Belfast: 13,600bhp

The *Medic*, seen here at Southampton Docks, and her sister *Megantic* were the first Shaw Savill cargo vessels to have full air-conditioning installed. They were also equipped with sewage treatment systems that could be employed in dock basins. In the early 1970s, as the Shaw Savill fleet began to contract in the face of foreign competition, the *Medic* and *Megantic* were deployed as Deck and Engineer Cadet training ships. This sustained them until 1979 when they were sold, the *Medic* passing to Greek owners Odysefs Shipping Corp, Piraeus, under the new name *Odysefs*. After eight more years trading, she was broken up in Pakistan in 1987. *Mick Lindsay*

ST ESSYLT

(6/1948) South American
Saint Line
6,855grt; 472ft 5in (143.99m)
loa x 59ft 7in (18.16m)
beam
J. L. Thompson & Sons Ltd,
Sunderland
Oil 2SA 5-cyl by William
Doxford & Sons Ltd,
Sunderland

The motor vessel *St. Essylt* and her sisters, *St. Thomas* and *St. John*, were strikingly modern in style for their time, exhibiting a rounded and faired bridge front with a squat, streamlined funnel. Hull lines, too, were sleek looking, featuring a curved and raked bow more typical of a modern passenger liner. The trend they introduced was simultaneously adopted by other companies, notably the Port Line in its *Port Auckland* and *Port Brisbane*, representing a swing to modernistic lines away from the squared lines and tall, cylindrical funnels of the past. The ships of the *St Essylt* class were radical in other respects too, being among the first cargo ships to have private, single-berth cabins for the entire crew, housed amidships above the main deck in the main accommodation block. Each ship could accommodate 12 passengers and carried 6 cadets. Registered in Cardiff, their owners' base port, the *St Essylt* and her sisters operated services from London, Hull and Antwerp to Brazil and River Plate ports. She is photographed here off Gravesend. The *St Essylt* was sold in 1965 to China Navigation Co Ltd (John Swire & Sons Ltd, London) and renamed *Yunnan*. She was sold again in 1971, becoming the *Lucky Two* of New Asia Steamship Co SA, Panama. After a further eight years of trading, she arrived at Kaohsiung on 23 January 1979 for scrapping. *Kenneth Wightman*

BALUCHISTAN

(5/1956) Strick Line (Frank C. Strick & Co Ltd)

8,370grt; 510ft 4in (155.54m) loa x 62ft 6in (19.05m) beam

John Readhead & Sons Ltd, North Shields

Oil 2SA 6-cyl Doxford by Wallsend Slipway Co, Wallsend-on-Tyne: 6,800bhp

Fourth ship of the name in the Strick fleet, the *Baluchistan* was launched on 15 December 1955, entering service five months later. From 1 May 1972 she and her sister *Baharistan* came under the management control of the P&O General Cargo Division (P&O had acquired a controlling interest in the Strick Line 10 years earlier, in October 1962). In the following year, on 19 April 1973, they were transferred to P&O ownership receiving the names *Strathairlie* and *Stratharos* respectively, two years, to the month, later. Surviving for a further two years until sold to Tien Cheng Steel Co, Kaohsiung for breaking up, the former *Baluchistan* arrived in Taiwan on 26 August 1977 for demolition to commence. *Mick Lindsay*

MURISTAN

(10/1950) Shahristan Steamship Co Ltd
8,408grt; 511ft 7in (155.92m) loa x 62ft 2in (18.95m)
   beam
John Readhead & Sons Ltd, North Shields
Triple-expansion 3-cyl steam reciprocating and double-
   reduction geared LP steam turbine with hydraulic
   coupling (by builder): 6,000ihp

An older Strick line cargo liner with a combination steam
power plant, the *Muristan* is shown berthed at the Tilbury
Cargo Jetty. Completed originally for the Strick Line, she
passed to the associated Shahristan Steamship Co in
1960. A series of ownership changes involving foreign
companies began in 1966 taking her first to Achille P.
Halcoussis of Greece for whom she was renamed *Leonis*.
Two years later she passed under the South Korean flag,
purchased by Korea Atlas Line and renamed *Atlas
Trader*. In 1970 she was acquired by Hualing Shipping
Corp, Liberia as the *Yaling* and two years after that she
was sold again, to the Chen Tung Shipping Co, also
Liberia. This final sale was not for continued trading,
however. Instead she was broken up by the Chi Shun
Hwa Steel Co, Kaohsiung from 17 May 1972.
Kenneth Wightman

ROTHESAY CASTLE

(6/1960) Union Castle Line

9,650grt; 519ft 10in (158.43m) loa x 66ft 1in (20.14m) beam

Greenock Dockyard Co, Greenock

Oil 2SA 6-cyl Doxford by Wallsend Slipway Co, Wallsend-on-Tyne: 9,500bhp

The general cargo ship *Rothesay Castle* and her sister, the *Rotherwick Castle*, were the culmination of a postwar rebuilding programme that in fact began even before World War 2 had ended, adding in total six new cargo vessels to the Union Castle fleet between 1946 and 1960. This pair, capable of 16 knots speed, operated the UK to Africa and USA routes. They were readily distinguished from other Union Castle 'R' boats by their short, high accommodation structure topped by a squat funnel with an angled top. The photograph shows the *Rothesay Castle* in December 1971. Four years after it was taken she was sold to Lloyd Uruguayo, Montevideo and renamed *Laura*.
Mick Lindsay

ROWALLAN CASTLE

(4/1943) Union Castle Line

7,950grt; 474ft 2in (144.52m) loa x 63ft 4in (19.30m) beam

Harland & Wolff, Belfast

Oil 2DA 8-cyl Burmeister & Wain (by builder): 9,375bhp

This delightful study of a refrigerated fruit ship, with gently rippling reflections in the foreground, shows the *Rowallan Castle* secured alongside at Cardiff in September 1970. She was the lead ship of a class of three vessels, entering service at the height of World War 2. Her sisters were the *Richmond Castle* and *Roxburgh Castle*, which also performed war duties. The trio featured the split-island configuration of accommodation structure favoured by British companies during this period. After serving Union Castle on a service from South Africa to UK and USA ports for 28 years, the *Rowallan Castle* was sold for breaking up in Taiwan in September 1971. *Mick Lindsay*

TINTAGEL CASTLE
(6/1954) Union Castle Line
7,447grt; 494ft 7in (150.74m) loa x 65ft 10in (20.06m)
   beam
Harland & Wolff, Belfast
Oil 2SA 8-cyl by Burmeister & Wain, Copenhagen:
   9,350bhp

One of a pair of shelter deck cargo vessels, with the *Tantallon Castle*, the *Tintagel Castle* maintained Union Castle's general cargo services between the UK, USA and South Africa for some 17 years. She is seen here, off the King George V Dock, London, on 8 March 1958. Thirteen years later, having become surplus to requirements, she was sold to Armar Shipping Co, Cyprus in October 1971 in a deal which took her sister to another Cypriot concern. The *Tintagel Castle* was renamed *Armar* and served her new owners until June 1978 when she was sold for demolition at Kaohsiung, Taiwan.
Kenneth Wightman

Front cover:
GLENFRUIN
(4/1948) ex *Astyanax* (1957) Glen Line
7,648grt; 487ft (148.43m) loa x 62ft 4in (19.00m) beam
Scott's S. B. & Eng. Co, Greenock:
Oil 2DA 8-cyl Burmeister & Wain by J. G. Kinkaid & Co, Greenock: 6,800bhp

Pictured off the Royal Docks in March 1961, the refrigerated cargo ship *Glenfruin* entered service as the Blue Funnel ship *Astyanax* (with China Mutual Navigation Co). She transferred to Glen Line ownership in November 1957 under a five-year charter. Duly returned to her former owners in September 1962, she continued in their service for a further 10 years reverting to her original Blue Funnel name. She was broken up at Kaohsiung, Taiwan from December 1972. *Kenneth Wightman*

Back cover:
WAIRANGI
(4/1942) ex *Empire Grace* (1946) Shaw Savill & Albion
13,478grt; 540ft (164.58m) loa x 70ft (21.33m) beam
Harland & Wolff, Belfast
2 x Oil 2DA 6-cyl Burmeister & Wain (by builder): 10,000bhp

Constructed during wartime as a nominal replacement for the first *Wairangi*, lost in the Pedestal convoy on 13 August 1942, and to a design based upon that of the *Waimerama* completed in 1938, the *Wairangi* first entered service as the Ministry of War Transport emergency-built cargo vessel *Empire Grace*. Pictured here in the Mersey Docks with an Alexandra Towing steam tug ahead of her, the *Wairangi* gave Shaw Savill 17 good years of service from the time when she passed into that company's ownership shortly after the war. She may be classed as a replacement Empire Food Ship but differed from earlier motorships of this type by being provided with accommodation space for 112 passengers. This was suppressed in 1951 and thereafter she functioned as a dedicated cargo liner. She grounded at Kloevholmen Island, near Stockholm, in 1963, suffering bottom damage. Little merit was to be gained from undertaking major, and expensive, repairs, so she was sold instead to be scrapped at Faslane, Scotland. Other emergency cargo vessels of this type were the *Empire Hope*, managed by Shaw Savill but lost on 12 August 1942, the *Empire Mercia* and the *Empire Wessex*. The latter pair metamorphosed for civilian operations into the *Empire Star* (Blue Star Line) and *Port Hobart* (Port Line) respectively. *Kenneth Wightman*

ACKNOWLEDGEMENTS
Bob Aspinall, Museum in Docklands
John Bartlett, World Ship Society Central Record
.David Clark
Justin Donald, Lloyd's Marine Intelligence Unit
Mick Lindsay
Port of London Authority
Southampton Central Library — Maritime & Special Collections

BIBLIOGRAPHY AND SOURCES
Ben Line by Graeme Somner (World Ship Society)
Blue Star by Tony Atkinson & Kevin O'Donoghue (World Ship Society)
Canadian Pacific by George Musk (World Ship Society)
Crossed Flags by W.A. Laxon, I. J. Farquhar, N. J. Kirby and F.W. Perry (World Ship Society)
Empire Food Ships by Richard de Kerbrech (Coach House Publications)
Frank C. Strick & Co by J. E. B. Belt and H. S. Appleyard (World Ship Society)
Liverpool Shipping by George Chandler (Phoenix House)
Merchant Fleets in Profile — various volumes by Duncan Haws (Patrick Stephens)
Merchant Ships — various by E.C. Talbot-Booth (Journal of Commerce)
Merchant Ships: World Built — various (Adlard Coles)
Modern Shipping Disasters, 1963-1987 by Norman Hooke (Lloyds of London Press)
Ocean Ships — various by H. M. Le Fleming or Bert Moody (Ian Allan Publishing)
P&O — A Fleet History by Stephen Rabson & Kevin O'Donoghue (World Ship Society)
Shaw Savill & Albion by Richard de Kerbrech (Conway Maritime)
The Ships That Serve New Zealand by I. G. Stewart (Reed, New Zealand)
The White Ships by R. M. Parsons (City of Bristol Museums & Art Gallery)
Lloyd's Registers

www.botacquaintances.co.uk
www.clydesite.co.uk/clydebuilt
www.red-duster.co.uk
www.ssmaritime.com
www.theshipslist.com